Antonio Scapellato

HACKERS & NERDS

Algorithmic Mindset

Mastering Algorithms for Creative Problem-Solving

Antonio Scapellato

HACKERS & NERDS

Algorithmic Mindset

Mastering Algorithms for
Creative Problem-Solving

Algorithmic Mindset

H&N

H&N

For the Better.

- Antonio Scapellato -

H&N

—— **Antonio Scapellato**

HACKERS & NERDS

Algorithmic Mindset

Mastering Algorithms for Creative Problem-Solving

hackersandnerds.com

H&N

Table of Contents

Introduction

In today's increasingly complex and interconnected world, the ability to think algorithmically has become a crucial skill. Whether you're solving a complex computational problem, making data-driven decisions, or seeking innovative solutions, having an algorithmic mindset can empower you to navigate the challenges of the digital age. Welcome to "Algorithmic Mindset," a comprehensive guide that will transform the way you approach problem-solving and decision-making.

Chapter by chapter, we will embark on a journey of exploration, starting with the fundamentals of algorithmic thinking and gradually diving into various problem-solving strategies, data structures, algorithm analysis, recursion, sorting and searching algorithms, graph algorithms, computational thinking, algorithm design patterns, ethical considerations, real-world applications, and nurturing an algorithmic mindset in your daily life.

In Chapter 1, "Introduction to Algorithmic Thinking," we lay the foundation by introducing you to the concept of algorithmic thinking and its significance in problem-solving. We explore the fundamental principles behind algorithms and their wide-ranging applications in various fields, from computer science to finance, healthcare to artificial intelligence.

Chapter 2, "Problem-Solving Strategies," takes you on a deep dive into different problem-solving strategies. You will discover powerful techniques such as divide and conquer, greedy algorithms, and dynamic programming. By understanding when and how to apply these strategies, you will unlock the potential to optimize your solutions and tackle complex problems efficiently.

Next, in Chapter 3, "Data Structures and Algorithms," we delve into the world of data structures. You will explore essential structures like arrays, linked lists, stacks, and queues and understand how they support efficient algorithm design and implementation. Armed with this knowledge, you will be equipped to choose the right data structure for each problem you encounter.

In Chapter 4, "Analyzing Algorithm Efficiency," we shift our focus to algorithm analysis and complexity theory. By learning how to measure and compare algorithm efficiency using Big O notation, you will gain insights into the performance characteristics of different algorithms and make informed choices when designing your solutions.

In Chapter 5, "Recursion and Backtracking," introduces you to the power of recursion and backtracking. These techniques are invaluable when dealing with complex problems that require breaking them down into smaller, solvable subproblems. You will understand the underlying concepts and witness their effectiveness through practical examples.

The journey continues in Chapter 6, "Parallel and Distributed Algorithms" Here, we dive into the exciting world of parallel and distributed algorithms, where we explore the cutting-edge techniques and strategies that allow us to scale our computations to unprecedented levels. As data volumes continue to grow exponentially and computational demands become increasingly complex, traditional sequential algorithms no longer suffice.

Chapter 7, "Graph Algorithms," takes you into the fascinating world of graphs. You will discover graph theory and its wide-ranging applications in various domains. Traversal algorithms, shortest path algorithms, and spanning tree algorithms are just a few of the topics we will explore. By the end of this chapter, you will have a solid understanding of how to analyze and solve problems involving graphs.

In Chapter 8, "Computational Thinking," we delve into the thought process that drives effective problem-solving. By developing computational thinking skills, you will learn how to break down complex problems into smaller, manageable tasks.

This chapter will equip you with a structured approach to tackle challenges and design efficient solutions.

Chapter 9, "Algorithm Design Patterns," introduces you to common algorithm design patterns. You will explore techniques such as divide and conquer, greedy algorithms, and dynamic programming. Understanding these patterns and knowing when to apply them can significantly improve your algorithmic solutions and help you solve problems more effectively.

Ethical considerations take center stage in Chapter 10, "Ethics and Algorithmic Bias." We delve into the profound impact algorithms have on society and discuss the ethical implications that arise. By exploring strategies to mitigate algorithmic bias and promote fairness, we aim to create a more responsible and inclusive algorithmic landscape.

Chapter 11, "Real-World Applications," bridges the gap between theory and practice. We examine how algorithmic thinking is applied in fields such as data science, artificial intelligence, cryptography, and more. Real-life examples and case studies will showcase the power of algorithms in driving innovation and shaping the world around us.

Finally, in Chapter 12, "Cultivating an Algorithmic Mindset," we reflect on the journey you have undertaken in developing an algorithmic mindset. We discuss strategies to continue nurturing and applying algorithmic thinking in your daily life.

By embracing this mindset, you can become a more effective problem-solver, decision-maker, and contributor to the advancement of society.

As you embark on this enlightening journey through the pages of "Algorithmic Mindset," I invite you to embrace the power of algorithms and unlock your full potential as a problem-solver. Whether you are a student, a professional, or an avid learner, the knowledge and skills you gain from this book will empower you to tackle challenges head-on, make informed decisions, and shape a better future.

So, let us dive in, explore the fascinating world of algorithms, and cultivate an algorithmic mindset that will serve as your compass in the digital age.

1

Introduction to Algorithmic Thinking

What is Algorithmic Thinking?

Algorithmic thinking is a powerful cognitive process that enables us to solve complex problems by breaking them down into smaller, manageable steps. It involves approaching challenges in a systematic and logical manner, employing a set of strategies to devise efficient solutions. Algorithmic thinking goes beyond simply finding a single answer; it focuses on developing a structured approach that can be applied to a wide range of problems.

To better understand algorithmic thinking, let's consider a real-life example: the development of navigation systems. In the not-so-distant past, finding the best route from one location to another often required a printed map and a lot of guesswork. However, with the advent of algorithms, navigating through unfamiliar territories has become significantly easier.

GPS devices and mapping applications now utilize sophisticated algorithms to calculate the optimal route based on various factors, such as traffic conditions, distance, and time constraints. These algorithms break down the problem of finding the best route into smaller steps: analyzing available data, considering multiple variables, and determining the most efficient path. By leveraging algorithmic thinking, these systems can provide accurate directions and adapt in real-time, revolutionizing the way we navigate and save time on our daily commutes.

Algorithmic thinking is not limited to computer science or technology-related fields. It has permeated numerous domains, including finance, healthcare, logistics, and even everyday decision-making. For instance, companies use algorithms to optimize supply chain management, hospitals employ algorithms to diagnose diseases and recommend treatments, and online platforms utilize algorithms to personalize user experiences.

By adopting an algorithmic thinking approach, individuals can enhance their problem-solving abilities. Algorithmic thinking encourages breaking down complex problems into smaller, manageable parts, identifying patterns, and designing step-by-step procedures to reach a solution. It involves developing a structured mindset that allows for iterative refinement and optimization of algorithms.

While algorithmic thinking may seem daunting at first, it is a skill that can be cultivated and refined over time.

By embracing this mindset, individuals gain the ability to tackle challenges with confidence and efficiency. In the upcoming sections, we will delve deeper into the principles and applications of algorithms, providing practical examples and exercises to develop algorithmic thinking skills.

Remember, algorithmic thinking is not limited to experts or computer scientists. It is a valuable tool that can empower individuals from various backgrounds to approach problems in a methodical and creative way. So, let's embark on this exciting journey of exploring the algorithmic mindset and discover how it can unlock our problem-solving potential.

The Significance of Algorithmic Thinking

In today's increasingly complex and interconnected world, algorithmic thinking has emerged as a crucial skill with significant implications for problem-solving and innovation. Its significance extends beyond the realms of computer science, permeating various fields and transforming the way we approach challenges.

To grasp the true significance of algorithmic thinking, let's take a look at a fascinating real-life story that showcases its transformative power. In 2012, a group of data scientists participated in a competition organized by Netflix, the popular online streaming service.

The challenge was to develop an algorithm that could accurately predict user movie preferences based on their previous viewing habits. The winning algorithm, developed by a team known as BellKor's Pragmatic Chaos, beat Netflix's own algorithm by a significant margin. This victory not only earned the team a $1 million prize but also highlighted the immense potential of algorithmic thinking in improving recommendation systems and personalizing user experiences.

Algorithmic thinking empowers us to tackle complex problems by breaking them down into smaller, more manageable components. By decomposing a problem and designing step-by-step procedures to solve it, we can navigate through intricate challenges more efficiently and arrive at effective solutions. This systematic approach enables us to identify patterns, analyze data, and make informed decisions based on logical reasoning.

The significance of algorithmic thinking becomes even more evident when we consider its applications in fields like finance, healthcare, and logistics. For example, algorithmic trading has revolutionized financial markets, enabling traders to make data-driven decisions and execute high-frequency trades with remarkable speed and accuracy. In healthcare, algorithms are being used to analyze medical data and assist in diagnosing diseases, leading to more precise and timely treatments. Furthermore, logistics companies utilize algorithms to optimize transportation routes, minimize costs, and enhance overall efficiency.

Beyond its immediate practical applications, algorithmic thinking also nurtures important cognitive skills. It encourages critical thinking, logical reasoning, and the ability to approach problems from multiple perspectives. Algorithmic thinkers learn to analyze complex systems, anticipate potential challenges, and devise strategies to overcome them. These skills are invaluable in today's rapidly evolving world, where adaptability and innovation are essential for success.

In an era dominated by data and technology, algorithmic thinking equips individuals with the ability to navigate the vast sea of information and extract meaningful insights. It empowers us to make informed decisions, solve problems efficiently, and unlock new possibilities for innovation. By adopting an algorithmic mindset, we can confront challenges head-on, leveraging data and logic to devise effective solutions.

Moreover, algorithmic thinking encourages a mindset of continuous improvement. As we encounter new problems, we can refine our algorithms, optimize our processes, and learn from the outcomes. This iterative approach allows us to constantly enhance our problem-solving skills and adapt to changing circumstances.

In the chapters that follow, we will delve deeper into the principles that underlie algorithms and explore their applications in various domains.

We will examine real-life case studies, engage in hands-on activities, and provide practical exercises to help you develop your algorithmic thinking skills. Whether you are a student, a professional, or simply someone seeking to sharpen their problem-solving abilities, embracing the algorithmic mindset will empower you to thrive in an increasingly algorithm-driven world.

So, let us embark on this exciting journey of discovering the potential of algorithmic thinking and uncover the transformative power it holds for problem-solving and innovation.

Principles of Algorithms

To truly understand the power of algorithmic thinking, we must explore the principles that underlie algorithms themselves. Algorithms are step-by-step procedures or sets of rules designed to solve specific problems or perform specific tasks. They form the backbone of computational processes and are the driving force behind the efficiency and effectiveness of many systems we encounter in our daily lives.

One of the fundamental principles of algorithms is their ability to break down complex problems into smaller, more manageable steps. This decomposition allows us to tackle intricate challenges by addressing each component individually. By dividing a problem into smaller subproblems, we can apply appropriate strategies to solve them and then combine the solutions to arrive at the desired outcome.

Consider the example of the traveling salesman problem (TSP), a classic algorithmic challenge. The task is to determine the shortest possible route a salesman should take to visit a set of cities and return to the starting point. The number of possible routes grows exponentially with the number of cities, making it computationally difficult to find the optimal solution for large-scale problems.

However, algorithms for the TSP employ a technique called divide and conquer. They divide the problem into smaller subproblems, finding the optimal route for subsets of cities and combining them to construct an overall solution. This decomposition and combination process significantly reduces the complexity of the problem, enabling efficient computation of solutions for practical scenarios.

Another key principle of algorithms is the use of logical reasoning and decision-making. Algorithms rely on a set of rules or conditions to guide their execution and determine the next steps. These rules are based on logical principles, allowing algorithms to make informed choices based on available data or specific criteria.

For instance, search algorithms, such as the popular binary search algorithm, employ a divide and conquer approach combined with logical decision-making. When searching for an item in a sorted list, the algorithm compares the target value with the middle element and narrows down the search space based on whether the target value is greater or smaller. By repetitively dividing the search space in half and making informed decisions, the algorithm quickly identifies the desired item with remarkable efficiency.

The principles of well-designed algorithms also include efficiency, correctness, and generality. Efficient algorithms strive to optimize time and resource usage, ensuring that solutions are achieved in a reasonable amount of time. Correctness ensures that the algorithm produces the expected output for all valid inputs. Generality refers to the ability of an algorithm to be applied to a wide range of problem instances, making it a versatile tool for problem-solving.

Understanding the principles of algorithms enables us to design and analyze effective solutions for a variety of problems. By following these principles, we can develop algorithms that are efficient, correct, and adaptable to different scenarios.

Efficiency is crucial when dealing with large datasets or time-critical tasks. Efficient algorithms minimize unnecessary computations and aim to solve problems in the most optimal way possible. For example, sorting algorithms like Quicksort and Merge Sort employ efficient techniques to rearrange elements in ascending or descending order with high speed and minimal resource usage.

Ensuring the correctness of an algorithm is vital to obtain reliable results. To achieve correctness, algorithms are designed to adhere to a set of predefined rules and conditions. Rigorous testing, formal proofs, and mathematical analysis are employed to verify the correctness of algorithms. This attention to detail and accuracy is what allows us to rely on algorithms to perform critical tasks in domains like medicine, finance, and transportation.

The generality of an algorithm is an essential aspect as well. Algorithms that can be applied to

a wide range of problem instances allow us to tackle diverse challenges with a unified approach. For example, graph algorithms, such as Dijkstra's algorithm for finding the shortest path, are applicable to various scenarios, including network routing, social network analysis, and transportation planning. This generality enhances the scalability and versatility of algorithms, making them valuable tools across different domains.

By grasping these principles and incorporating them into our algorithmic thinking, we can develop effective solutions and optimize problem-solving processes. In the following chapters, we will explore practical examples and engage in hands-on activities to further strengthen our understanding of algorithmic principles. So, let us delve deeper into the world of algorithms and unlock the immense potential they hold for problem-solving and innovation.

Applications of Algorithms in Various Fields

Algorithms are not confined to the realms of computer science and technology; they have a far-reaching impact across a multitude of fields. From finance to healthcare, algorithms play a vital role in optimizing processes, making predictions, and enabling innovation. Let's explore some fascinating examples that highlight the broad applications of algorithms in diverse domains.

Finance

In the world of finance, algorithms have transformed the way trading and investment decisions are made. High-frequency trading algorithms analyze vast amounts of market data in real-time, identifying patterns and executing trades with lightning speed. These algorithms leverage complex mathematical models and statistical analysis to exploit fleeting market opportunities and generate profits. Their ability to process and respond to data faster than human traders has reshaped financial markets and led to more efficient and dynamic trading environments.

Healthcare

Algorithms are revolutionizing healthcare by enhancing diagnostics, treatment planning, and patient care. In medical imaging, algorithms can analyze radiographic images, detect anomalies, and assist radiologists in making accurate diagnoses. For example, deep learning algorithms have demonstrated remarkable accuracy in detecting early signs of diseases like cancer from medical images, enabling timely interventions and potentially saving lives.

Algorithms also contribute to precision medicine by analyzing genetic data and identifying personalized treatment options. By considering an individual's genetic makeup, medical history, and environmental factors, algorithms can help physicians determine the most effective treatment protocols for patients, optimizing outcomes and reducing adverse effects.

Logistics and Transportation
Efficient transportation and logistics are critical for businesses and society at large. Algorithms play a key role in optimizing routes, minimizing costs, and improving overall efficiency. For instance, logistics companies utilize algorithms to solve the vehicle routing problem, determining the most efficient routes for delivery trucks while considering factors such as traffic conditions, package sizes, and delivery deadlines. These algorithms reduce fuel consumption, improve delivery times, and enhance customer satisfaction.

Social Media and Recommendation Systems
Algorithms power the recommendation systems we encounter on social media platforms, online marketplaces, and streaming services. These systems analyze user preferences, behaviors, and interactions to deliver personalized recommendations. For example, the algorithms behind YouTube's recommendation system

analyze billions of data points to suggest relevant videos, keeping users engaged and driving content discovery.

Similarly, e-commerce platforms leverage algorithms to provide tailored product recommendations based on customers' browsing and purchase histories. This personalization enhances user experience, increases customer satisfaction, and drives sales.

Natural Language Processing and Artificial Intelligence
Algorithms are at the core of natural language processing (NLP) and artificial intelligence (AI) technologies. NLP algorithms enable machines to understand and interpret human language, facilitating tasks such as language translation, sentiment analysis, and chatbot interactions. Voice assistants like Siri, Alexa, and Google Assistant utilize NLP algorithms to process spoken commands and provide relevant responses.

AI algorithms encompass a wide range of applications, including image recognition, autonomous vehicles, and virtual assistants. These algorithms learn from data, identify patterns, and make predictions or decisions based on that learning. The advancements in AI algorithms have led to breakthroughs in areas such as computer vision, natural language understanding, and robotics.

These examples only scratch the surface of the vast applications of algorithms in various fields. As technology continues to evolve, algorithms will continue to play an increasingly important role in shaping our lives, driving innovation, and addressing complex challenges.

The power of algorithms lies in their ability to process and analyze large volumes of data, identify patterns, and make informed decisions or recommendations. By leveraging algorithms, businesses can gain valuable insights, optimize processes, and make data-driven decisions. Individuals can benefit from personalized experiences, improved healthcare, and more efficient services.

As we continue our exploration of the algorithmic mindset, it becomes evident that understanding and harnessing the potential of algorithms is essential in today's data-driven world. By embracing algorithmic thinking and staying abreast of advancements in algorithm design and application, we can unlock new possibilities, solve complex problems, and drive innovation in our respective fields.

In the subsequent chapters, we will delve deeper into specific algorithmic concepts, explore practical examples, and engage in hands-on activities to sharpen our algorithmic thinking skills. So, let us continue this enlightening journey and unlock the transformative power of algorithms in problem-solving and beyond.

Ethical Considerations in Algorithmic Thinking

As we delve deeper into the world of algorithms and their applications, it is crucial to address the ethical considerations that arise when harnessing the power of algorithmic thinking. While algorithms bring tremendous benefits, they also pose potential risks and challenges that must be carefully navigated.

One key ethical consideration is algorithmic bias. Algorithms are created by humans, and they can inadvertently perpetuate biases and discrimination present in the data used to train them. Real-life incidents have shed light on the impact of biased algorithms in various domains. For instance, in the field of criminal justice, algorithms used for risk assessment have been found to exhibit racial bias, leading to disproportionately harsher treatment for certain racial and ethnic groups. These biases can amplify existing inequalities and perpetuate social injustices.

Another ethical concern is privacy and data security. Algorithms rely on vast amounts of data to make informed decisions and predictions. However, the collection, storage, and use of personal data raise concerns about privacy and data security. Cases of data breaches and misuse have highlighted the need for stringent safeguards to protect individuals' sensitive information. Striking a balance between leveraging data for algorithmic advancements and safeguarding privacy is essential to maintain public trust and uphold ethical standards.

Transparency and accountability are also vital in algorithmic decision-making. When algorithms influence critical decisions that impact individuals' lives, it becomes crucial to ensure transparency in how these algorithms operate. People should have a clear understanding of the factors considered and the reasoning behind algorithmic decisions. Additionally, mechanisms should be in place to hold algorithm creators accountable for any potential biases, errors, or unintended consequences that may arise.

To address these ethical considerations, researchers and practitioners are actively exploring techniques such as algorithmic auditing, fairness-aware machine learning, and the development of ethical guidelines for algorithmic design and implementation. These endeavors aim to mitigate bias, promote transparency, and establish frameworks for responsible algorithmic development.

As algorithmic thinkers, we have a responsibility to critically examine the ethical implications of our work. By adopting an ethical mindset, we can actively address these considerations and work towards creating algorithms that are fair, transparent, and accountable.

In the following chapters, we will explore ethical considerations in algorithm design, data usage, and decision-making. We will examine case studies and real-world examples that highlight the impact of algorithmic bias and the importance of responsible algorithm development. By integrating ethical principles into our algorithmic thinking, we can contribute to a more equitable and inclusive technological landscape.

Thinking, recognizing the power we hold as algorithm creators and the impact our decisions can have on individuals and society as a whole. By upholding ethical standards, we can harness the full potential of algorithms while ensuring a just and responsible application of algorithmic thinking.

The Future of Algorithmic Thinking

As we stand at the forefront of technological advancements, the future of algorithmic thinking holds immense potential and exciting possibilities. Emerging technologies such as artificial intelligence (AI), machine learning, and quantum computing are reshaping the landscape of algorithm design and application. Let's explore some of the key areas where algorithmic thinking is set to make a significant impact in the years to come.

Artificial Intelligence and Machine Learning

Artificial intelligence, fueled by machine learning algorithms, is rapidly advancing and transforming various industries. Machine learning algorithms learn from data, identify patterns, and make predictions or decisions without being explicitly programmed. The integration of AI and machine learning into our daily lives is evident through voice assistants, personalized recommendations, and autonomous vehicles.

In healthcare, AI-powered algorithms hold great promise. They can analyze large volumes of medical data, identify disease patterns, and assist in diagnosis. For instance, researchers at Stanford University developed an algorithm that can detect skin cancer with an accuracy comparable to expert dermatologists. Such advancements have the potential to improve healthcare outcomes and accessibility on a global scale.

Quantum Computing

Quantum computing, an emerging field with the potential to revolutionize computing capabilities, relies heavily on algorithmic thinking. Quantum algorithms exploit the principles of quantum mechanics to solve complex problems more efficiently than classical algorithms. They hold the promise of solving optimization problems, simulating quantum systems, and breaking current encryption methods.

One notable example is Shor's algorithm, a quantum algorithm that can factor large numbers exponentially faster than classical algorithms. If scalable quantum computers become a reality, Shor's algorithm could pose a significant threat to modern encryption systems. This highlights the need for algorithmic advancements to develop quantum-resistant encryption methods.

Internet of Things (IoT)

The proliferation of connected devices in the Internet of Things (IoT) ecosystem generates massive amounts of data. Algorithmic thinking plays a crucial role in extracting meaningful insights from this data and enabling efficient communication and decision-making. Algorithms for data processing, pattern recognition, and predictive analysis are vital for maximizing the potential of IoT technologies.

Smart cities, for example, leverage IoT devices and algorithms to optimize resource usage, improve traffic management, and enhance public safety. Algorithms analyze data from sensors and devices to make real-time decisions that optimize energy consumption, reduce congestion, and predict potential safety risks.

Computational Creativity
Algorithmic thinking is not limited to problem-solving; it is also extending its reach into the realm of creativity. Computational creativity explores the intersection of algorithms and human creativity, enabling the generation of novel ideas, artistic creations, and musical compositions.

For instance, algorithms can analyze vast amounts of existing music compositions to generate new melodies and harmonies, providing inspiration to musicians and composers. Similarly, algorithms can analyze patterns in visual art to generate unique and aesthetically pleasing designs. These algorithmic creations can serve as a starting point for human artists and inspire new forms of artistic expression.

The future of algorithmic thinking is intertwined with the continuous advancement of technology. As we explore the potential of AI, quantum computing, IoT, and computational creativity, it is crucial to address the ethical considerations and social impact that accompany these advancements.

Responsible algorithmic thinking should always be guided by ethical principles and a focus on the greater good.

In the upcoming chapters, we will delve deeper into specific applications of algorithmic thinking in these emerging fields. We will explore cutting-edge research, real-life case studies, and the ethical implications associated with these advancements

. By embracing the future of algorithmic thinking, we can drive innovation, solve complex challenges, and shape a better tomorrow.

Let us embark on this exciting journey into the future, where algorithmic thinking continues to evolve and transform the way we live, work, and create.

2

Problem-Solving Strategies

In today's increasingly complex and interconnected world, the ability to think algorithmically has become a crucial skill. Whether you're solving a complex computational problem, making data-driven decisions, or seeking innovative solutions, having an algorithmic mindset can empower you to navigate the challenges of the digital age. Welcome to "Algorithmic Mindset," a comprehensive guide that will transform the way you approach problem-solving and decision-making.

Chapter by chapter, we will embark on a journey of exploration, starting with the fundamentals of algorithmic thinking and gradually diving into various problem-solving strategies, data structures, algorithm analysis, recursion, sorting and searching algorithms, graph algorithms, computational thinking, algorithm design patterns, ethical considerations, real-world applications, and nurturing an algorithmic mindset in your daily life.

Divide and Conquer: Breaking Down Complex Problems

In the world of problem-solving, the divide and conquer strategy is a powerful tool for tackling complex problems by breaking them down into smaller, more manageable subproblems. This approach allows us to focus on solving each subproblem independently, eventually combining their solutions to solve the larger problem at hand. Let's delve into the intricacies of this strategy and explore its applications and benefits.

The divide and conquer strategy follows three fundamental steps: divide, conquer, and combine. Firstly, the problem is divided into smaller subproblems that are similar in nature to the original problem but easier to solve. Then, we conquer each subproblem by solving them recursively or through other problem-solving strategies. Finally, we combine the solutions of the subproblems to obtain the solution to the original problem.

One classic example of the divide and conquer strategy is the Merge Sort algorithm. This sorting algorithm works by dividing an array into two halves, sorting each half individually, and then merging the sorted halves to obtain the final sorted array. By dividing the sorting task into smaller subproblems and conquering them individually, Merge Sort achieves a time complexity of O(n log n) and is widely used in practice.

Another real-life application of divide and conquer can be

seen in efficient web search algorithms. Search engines break down the search query into smaller keywords, search each keyword independently, and then combine the results to provide the most relevant search results to the user. This approach allows search engines to efficiently process vast amounts of data and deliver search results in a matter of seconds.

Divide and conquer also finds applications in computational geometry. Algorithms such as Quickhull and Graham's scan, used for computing convex hulls, employ the divide and conquer strategy. These algorithms divide the set of points into smaller subsets, solve each subset recursively, and then combine the results to obtain the convex hull of the entire set of points. This approach significantly reduces the time complexity of the problem and enables efficient computations in geometric applications.

While the divide and conquer strategy offers numerous benefits, it is essential to consider its limitations. Dividing the problem into smaller subproblems incurs additional overhead, and combining the solutions may introduce complexities. Additionally, not all problems can be effectively solved using the divide and conquer strategy, as some problems may lack the necessary characteristics for this approach to be efficient.

By mastering the divide and conquer strategy, you can effectively break down complex problems into manageable pieces and design efficient algorithms. This approach empowers you to tackle challenges that may initially seem overwhelming. As we proceed to explore other problem-solving strategies, keep in mind the power of divide and conquer and how it can be applied to various domains.

Greedy Algorithms: Making Optimal Choices

In the realm of problem-solving, the greedy algorithmic strategy offers a fascinating approach to optimization problems. Greedy algorithms make locally optimal choices at each step with the hope that these choices will lead to a globally optimal solution. Let's dive into the world of greedy algorithms, understand how they work, and explore their applications in real-life scenarios.

The essence of the greedy approach lies in making the best choice at each step without considering the overall consequences. By selecting the most favorable option at each decision point, greedy algorithms aim to achieve the best possible solution. However, it's important to note that the greedy strategy does not guarantee an optimal solution for every problem.

One classic example of a greedy algorithm is the Knapsack Problem. Imagine you have a knapsack with a limited capacity and a set of items, each with a value and weight. The goal is to maximize the total value of the items you can fit into the knapsack without exceeding its capacity. A greedy approach to this problem involves sorting the items based on their value-to-weight ratio and adding items to the knapsack in descending order of this ratio until the capacity is reached. While this approach may not always result in the absolute optimal solution, it often provides a reasonably good solution in a computationally efficient manner.

Greedy algorithms find numerous applications in real-world scenarios. One compelling example is the Minimum Spanning Tree (MST) problem in graph theory. In this problem, the goal is to find the most cost-effective way to connect all the nodes in a weighted graph. The greedy algorithm known as Kruskal's algorithm follows a step-by-step approach of selecting the shortest edge that does not form a cycle until all the nodes are connected. This algorithm efficiently solves the MST problem and has practical applications in network design, logistics planning, and communication networks.

Another real-life application of greedy algorithms is seen in Dijkstra's algorithm for finding the shortest path in a graph. By making locally optimal choices at each step, Dijkstra's algorithm efficiently computes the shortest path from a starting node to all other nodes in a graph. This algorithm finds extensive use in navigation systems, network routing protocols, and resource allocation optimization.

While the greedy strategy offers simplicity and efficiency, it's important to be aware of its limitations. Greedy algorithms may sometimes lead to suboptimal solutions as they do not consider the global picture and focus solely on immediate gains. Certain problems may require alternative strategies or additional considerations to guarantee the optimal solution. By mastering the greedy algorithmic strategy, you can efficiently solve optimization problems and make optimal choices in various domains. Understanding the principles of the greedy approach empowers you to identify scenarios where this strategy is applicable and determine its feasibility for achieving near-optimal solutions. As we proceed to explore other problem-solving strategies, remember the power of greedy algorithms and their potential to optimize decision-making processes in real-life situations.

Dynamic Programming: Solving Overlapping Subproblems

Dynamic programming, a problem-solving technique that solves subproblems once and reuses their solutions, offers a powerful approach to tackling complex problems. By breaking down a problem into smaller overlapping subproblems and efficiently combining their solutions, dynamic programming can optimize solutions and provide significant computational advantages. Let's delve into the world of dynamic programming, understand its underlying principles, and explore its real-life applications.

At the core of dynamic programming lies the concept of optimal substructure, which states that an optimal solution to a problem can be constructed from optimal solutions to its subproblems. Dynamic programming leverages this concept and solves each subproblem only once, storing the solution for future reference. By reusing these solutions, dynamic programming avoids redundant computations and significantly improves the efficiency of the algorithm. One classic example that showcases the power of dynamic programming is the Fibonacci sequence. The Fibonacci sequence is defined as a series of numbers where each number is the sum of the two preceding numbers: 0, 1, 1, 2, 3, 5, 8, 13, and so on. Calculating Fibonacci numbers using a naive approach can be computationally expensive, as the same subproblems are solved repeatedly. However, by utilizing dynamic programming, we can store the solutions to each subproblem and retrieve them when needed, reducing the computational complexity to linear time.

Another real-life application of dynamic programming is the Longest Common Subsequence (LCS) problem. In this problem, given two sequences, the goal is to find the longest subsequence that is common to both sequences. A subsequence is a sequence that can be derived from another sequence by deleting some or no elements without changing the order of the remaining elements. Dynamic programming provides an efficient solution to this problem by breaking it down into smaller subproblems and reusing their solutions to construct the LCS. This approach has applications in DNA sequence analysis, text comparison, and version control systems.

Dynamic programming also finds applications in the field of robotics and motion planning. Algorithms that compute optimal paths or trajectories for robots, taking into account constraints and obstacles, often employ dynamic programming. By breaking down the problem into smaller subproblems and reusing their solutions, these algorithms can quickly find efficient paths for robots to navigate in complex environments.

Dynamic programming offers a powerful approach to solving problems with overlapping substructures. By efficiently reusing solutions to subproblems, dynamic programming can optimize computations and provide significant performance improvements. As we explore different problem-solving strategies, remember the potential of dynamic programming and its real-life applications. By mastering this technique, you can design efficient algorithms that solve complex problems and optimize decision-making processes in various domains.

Backtracking: Exploring All Possibilities

In the realm of problem-solving, the backtracking strategy offers a versatile approach to exploring all possible solutions to a problem by systematically searching through the problem space. This strategy allows us to backtrack or undo certain decisions when we realize they will not lead to a valid or optimal solution. Let's delve into the world of backtracking, understand its principles, and explore its applications in various real-life scenarios.

Backtracking involves a systematic search through the problem space, considering different possibilities at each step and carefully examining their consequences. It explores one path at a time and backtracks when necessary, discarding partial solutions that cannot be extended to a valid solution. This approach is particularly useful for solving problems where exhaustive exploration of all possibilities is required.

One example that showcases the power of backtracking is the N-Queens problem. In this problem, the goal is to place N queens on an N×N chessboard such that no two queens threaten each other. Backtracking allows us to systematically explore different configurations, placing queens one by one and checking if they are in conflict with each other. If a conflict arises, backtracking occurs, and the algorithm explores alternative possibilities. This process continues until a valid solution is found or all possibilities have been exhausted.

Another real-life application of backtracking can be seen in Sudoku solving algorithms. Sudoku puzzles present a grid that must be filled with digits in such a way that each column, each row, and each of the nine 3×3 subgrids contains all the digits from 1 to 9 without repetition. Backtracking algorithms effectively solve Sudoku puzzles by iteratively placing digits in empty cells and backtracking when a conflict occurs. This process continues until a valid solution is found or all possibilities are explored.

Backtracking is also widely used in the field of computer graphics and computer games. In computer graphics, algorithms may employ backtracking to generate and explore different paths in a virtual environment to simulate realistic movement or interactions. In computer games, backtracking can be used for AI pathfinding, where the algorithm explores different paths to find the optimal route for characters or game agents. Backtracking offers a powerful strategy for exploring all possibilities in a problem space, allowing us to find valid solutions or make informed decisions. By systematically traversing the problem space and backtracking when necessary, backtracking algorithms can efficiently search for solutions even in complex scenarios. As we explore different problem-solving strategies, remember the versatility of backtracking and its applications in various domains. Mastering this technique will equip you with the skills to solve challenging problems that require exhaustive exploration of all possibilities.

Heuristics: Finding Approximate Solutions

In the world of problem-solving, heuristics offer a practical and efficient approach to finding approximate solutions when an optimal solution is either computationally expensive or not feasible. Heuristics are strategies or techniques that provide shortcuts or rules of thumb to guide decision-making processes. Let's dive into the realm of heuristics, understand their principles, and explore their applications in real-life scenarios.

Heuristics are designed to find solutions that are close to optimal, even though they may not guarantee the absolute best solution. They are particularly useful when solving complex problems that have a large search space or involve a high computational cost to explore all possibilities.

Heuristics enable us to make informed decisions based on incomplete information, constraints, or predefined rules.

One classic example that showcases the power of heuristics is the Traveling Salesman Problem (TSP). The TSP is a well-known optimization problem that aims to find the shortest possible route that visits a set of cities exactly once and returns to the starting city. Finding the optimal solution to the TSP is computationally demanding, especially as the number of cities increases. Heuristics such as the Nearest Neighbor algorithm and the 2-Opt algorithm provide efficient approaches to finding near-optimal solutions by making informed decisions based on local information and heuristics-specific rules.

In real-life scenarios, heuristics find applications in various fields. For example, in route planning and navigation systems, heuristics are used to find approximate routes between locations based on factors like distance, traffic conditions, and historical data. These algorithms prioritize efficiency and provide reasonably good solutions for daily commute or delivery route optimization.

Heuristics are also utilized in resource allocation problems, such as scheduling tasks in project management. Algorithms based on heuristics help determine the best allocation of resources to minimize project completion time or cost. These algorithms consider factors like task dependencies, resource availability, and estimated durations to make informed decisions and achieve efficient resource allocation.

Additionally, heuristics are employed in machine learning and optimization algorithms. Metaheuristic algorithms, such as genetic algorithms and simulated annealing, use heuristics to explore the solution space and find near-optimal solutions in complex optimization problems. These algorithms are inspired by natural processes, such as evolution or cooling systems, and offer efficient solutions for problems that are difficult to solve using exact methods.

Heuristics provide practical and efficient approaches to problem-solving, allowing us to find approximate solutions when optimal solutions are challenging to obtain. By leveraging rules of thumb, shortcuts, and heuristics-specific techniques, we can navigate complex problem spaces and make informed decisions. As we explore different problem-solving strategies, remember the power of heuristics and their potential to provide practical solutions in real-life scenarios. Mastering the art of heuristics equips you with valuable tools to find near-optimal solutions and make efficient decisions in various domains.

Randomized Algorithms: Embracing Uncertainty

In the realm of problem-solving, randomized algorithms offer an intriguing approach that embraces uncertainty and randomness to find solutions. These algorithms introduce an element of randomness in their execution, which allows them to efficiently solve problems or make decisions in situations where deterministic approaches may be impractical or less effective. Let's dive into the world of randomized algorithms, understand their principles, and explore their real-life applications.

Randomized algorithms incorporate random choices or random input to solve problems. While randomness may seem counterintuitive when seeking precise solutions, it can be remarkably effective in certain scenarios. By leveraging randomness, these algorithms can provide probabilistic guarantees of finding approximate solutions or achieving desirable properties.

One classic example that showcases the power of randomized algorithms is the QuickSort algorithm. QuickSort is a popular sorting algorithm that employs a randomized partitioning strategy. It randomly selects a pivot element and partitions the input array into two parts, ensuring that elements smaller than the pivot are on the left, and elements greater than the pivot are on the right. The algorithm then recursively applies this process to the subarrays until the entire array is sorted. The random choice of the pivot helps QuickSort achieve an average-case time complexity of O(n log n) and makes it highly efficient in practice.

Real-life scenarios often present challenges where randomized algorithms find applications. One such application is in network routing protocols. Randomized algorithms can be employed to determine the optimal route for data packets in a network, especially in situations where the network topology changes dynamically. These algorithms introduce randomness in the routing decisions to distribute the network load efficiently and adapt to changing network conditions.

Another real-life application of randomized algorithms is seen in cryptography. Randomness plays a vital role in generating secure cryptographic keys. Randomized algorithms are used to generate random numbers or sequences that form the basis of cryptographic key generation, enhancing the security of communication systems and data encryption.

Randomized algorithms also find applications in machine learning and data analysis. Algorithms such as Random Forest and Monte Carlo methods utilize randomness to improve prediction accuracy, handle uncertainty, and make informed decisions based on probabilistic models. These algorithms are widely used in areas such as pattern recognition, data clustering, and simulation.

Randomized algorithms embrace the element of uncertainty and leverage randomness to solve complex problems efficiently. By incorporating random choices or random input, these algorithms offer practical solutions, probabilistic guarantees, and improved performance in certain scenarios. As we explore different problem-solving strategies, remember the power of randomized algorithms and their real-life applications. Mastering these techniques equips you with the ability to tackle challenging problems, make informed decisions, and harness the potential of randomness to your advantage.

DNA	Machine Code
AT	0x00624020
GC	0x01004020
GT	0xad0f0010
AC	0x018c7020
GT	0x01004020
AC	0xad100014
GA	0x00624820
CT	0x01004020
AG	0xad110018
CT	0x00625020
GA	0x01004020
CG	0xad12001c
AT	0x018c7020
CG	0x01004020
AT	0xad130020
CG	0x00624020

3

Data Structures and Algorithms

Arrays: Efficient Data Storage and Access

Arrays are one of the fundamental data structures in computer science, offering efficient storage and access to elements. Imagine a shelf filled with labeled boxes, each containing an item. This simple analogy can help us understand the concept of arrays. In an array, elements are stored in contiguous memory locations, and each element can be accessed using its index.

Arrays provide several advantages in terms of data storage and access. Firstly, they offer constant-time access to any element by using its index, allowing for direct retrieval without the need for traversal. This feature makes arrays efficient for scenarios where fast element retrieval is crucial, such as searching for specific values or accessing elements in mathematical computations.

Let's explore a real-life example to illustrate the power of arrays. Consider a music streaming application that needs to store a playlist of songs. An array can be used to represent the playlist, with each element in the array representing a song. The index of each song in the array allows for quick and direct access to any song in the playlist. Whether the user wants to play the first song or jump to the middle of the playlist, the array enables efficient retrieval and playback.

Arrays also support various operations, such as insertion and deletion. However, these operations can be less efficient than accessing elements due to the need for shifting or resizing the array. For example, if a new song needs to be added to the playlist, the array may need to be resized, requiring memory allocation and element relocation. Similarly, if a song is removed from the playlist, the array may need to be adjusted by shifting elements to fill the empty space. These operations can have a time complexity proportional to the number of elements in the array, affecting the overall performance.

Despite these limitations, arrays find extensive use in many real-world applications. They are employed in image and audio processing, scientific computations, and data storage systems, among others. Their efficient access pattern and predictable memory layout make arrays indispensable for tasks that require fast and direct element retrieval.

Arrays provide a powerful foundation for efficient data storage and access. By leveraging their ability to directly access elements using indices, arrays offer fast retrieval and manipulation of data. Understanding how arrays work and their advantages and limitations equips you with the necessary knowledge to leverage this data structure effectively. As we continue our exploration of data structures and algorithms, remember the significance of arrays and their applications in diverse fields.

Array

12	43	99	897	32	16

Linked Lists: Dynamic Data Organization

In the world of data structures, linked lists provide a dynamic and flexible way of organizing data. Unlike arrays, which have a fixed size and require contiguous memory allocation, linked lists allow for efficient insertion and deletion operations by dynamically allocating memory for each element. Let's delve into the fascinating world of linked lists, understand their unique characteristics, and explore their real-life applications.

Imagine a chain of interconnected blocks where each block contains data and a reference to the next block. This analogy helps us visualize a linked list. In a linked list, elements, called nodes, are connected through pointers or references, forming a linear sequence. Each node contains the data it holds and a reference to the next node in the list.

One of the key advantages of linked lists is their ability to accommodate dynamic resizing and insertion operations. Suppose you want to create a to-do list application that allows users to add tasks dynamically. A linked list would be an ideal choice for this scenario. Each task can be represented as a node, and new tasks can be easily added by creating a new node and updating the reference of the previous node to point to the new node. This dynamic resizing feature of linked lists makes them suitable for scenarios where the number of elements is unpredictable or frequently changing.

Linked lists also excel in scenarios where efficient insertion and deletion at arbitrary positions are required. Consider a scenario where you are implementing a text editor that supports undo and redo operations. Linked lists can be used to implement a stack-like behavior, where each node represents a state of the text document. When an undo operation is performed, the previous state can be easily restored by traversing the linked list and updating the reference to the current node.

However, linked lists do have some limitations. Unlike arrays, which allow for direct access to elements using indices, linked lists require traversal from the beginning to reach a specific node. This traversal can result in increased time complexity, especially for large lists. Additionally, linked lists consume more memory than arrays due to the overhead of storing references or pointers for each node.

Despite these limitations, linked lists find practical applications in various domains. They are commonly used in operating systems for managing process control blocks, in file systems for managing file directories, and in networking protocols for managing packets, to name a few examples.

Linked lists provide a dynamic and flexible approach to data organization, enabling efficient insertion and deletion operations. By understanding the unique characteristics of linked lists and their real-life applications, you gain valuable insights into their usefulness and versatility. As we continue our exploration of data structures and algorithms, keep in mind the power of linked lists and their ability to handle dynamic scenarios with ease.

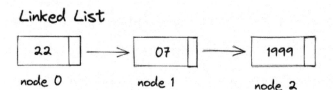

Linked List

node 0   node 1   node 2

Stacks: Last-In-First-Out Data Structure

In the world of data structures, stacks represent a fascinating concept known as Last-In-First-Out (LIFO). Picture a stack of plates in a buffet restaurant, where the last plate placed on the stack is the first one to be taken off. This analogy helps us understand the behavior of stacks, a data structure widely used in various applications.

A stack is a collection of elements that follows a strict LIFO order. It offers two primary operations: push and pop. When an element is pushed onto the stack, it is added to the top, becoming the most recently inserted element. Conversely, when an element is popped from the stack, the top element is removed and accessed. The stack

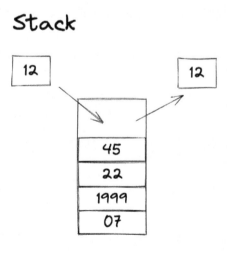

operates in such a way that only the top element is accessible, while the other elements remain hidden beneath.

Stacks find real-life analogies and applications in many scenarios. Let's consider a practical example of a web browser's back button functionality. When you navigate through different web pages, the browser maintains a stack-like structure of the visited pages. Each time you visit a new page, it is pushed onto the stack. If you click the back button, the most recently visited page is popped from the stack, allowing you to navigate back to the previous page. This behavior follows the LIFO principle of stacks and provides an intuitive and efficient way to track and manage page navigation history.

The LIFO behavior of stacks makes them particularly useful in managing function calls within computer programs. When a function is called, its execution context is pushed onto the stack, including variables, parameters, and the return address. As the function completes its execution, its context is popped from the stack, and the program returns to the point of the original function call. This mechanism ensures that the execution flow follows the correct order of function calls and returns, enabling efficient program execution and memory management.

Stacks can be implemented using various underlying data structures, such as arrays or linked lists. While arrays offer constant-time access to elements, linked lists provide flexibility in terms of dynamic resizing. The choice of implementation depends on the specific requirements and constraints of the application.

Stacks, with their Last-In-First-Out behavior, offer a simple yet powerful approach to data management. By understanding their real-life analogies and applications, you gain a deeper appreciation for the role of stacks in various domains. As we continue our exploration of data structures and algorithms, remember the versatility of stacks and how they can facilitate efficient function call management, web navigation history, and more.

Queues: First-In-First-Out Data Structure

In the realm of data structures, queues represent an intriguing concept known as First-In-First-Out (FIFO). Imagine waiting in line at a ticket counter, where the person who arrives first is served first. This analogy helps us grasp the behavior of queues, a data structure widely used in diverse applications.

A queue is a collection of elements that follows a strict FIFO order. It supports two primary operations: enqueue and dequeue. When an element is enqueued, it is added to the back of the queue, becoming the last element. Conversely, when an element is dequeued, the front element is removed and accessed. The queue operates in such a way that the elements are processed in the same order they were added, resembling a real-world line or queue.

Queues find real-life applications and analogies in numerous scenarios. Consider a bank with multiple teller windows and a single queue for customers. As customers arrive, they join the back of the queue. When a teller becomes available, the customer at the front of the queue is served, following the FIFO principle. This arrangement ensures fair and orderly customer service, preventing any individual from being repeatedly served before others.

Another practical example of queues can be found in network packet routing. In computer networks, packets of data traverse various routers to reach their destination. Queues are used at each router to temporarily store incoming packets. As packets arrive, they are enqueued, and when a router is ready to process a packet, it dequeues the front packet from its queue. This ensures that packets are processed in the order they were received, preventing delays and maintaining the integrity of the data flow.

Queues can be implemented using various underlying data structures, such as arrays or linked lists. Each implementation offers its advantages and considerations. Arrays provide fast access to both ends of the queue but may require resizing if the number of elements exceeds the initial capacity. On the other hand, linked lists offer dynamic resizing but require traversal for accessing the back of the queue.

Queues, with their First-In-First-Out behavior, provide a structured and efficient way to manage data. By understanding their real-life applications and analogies, you gain insights into how queues facilitate fair service, data routing, and orderly processing. As we delve further into the realm of data structures and algorithms, remember the significance of queues and how they can streamline processes in a wide range of domains.

Queue

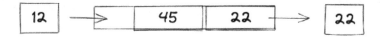

Trees: Hierarchical Data Structure

In the realm of data structures, trees represent a fascinating hierarchical structure that mimics the organization of many natural systems. Imagine a family tree, with ancestors, parents, and descendants interconnected through branches. This analogy helps us grasp the essence of trees, a versatile data structure with numerous real-life applications.

A tree is a collection of nodes connected in a hierarchical manner. It consists of a root node at the top, which serves as the starting point, and subsequent nodes arranged in levels, forming branches or subtrees. Each node in a tree can have zero or more child nodes, and each child node can have its own set of children, creating a hierarchical structure.

Trees find practical applications in various domains. Let's consider a file system as an example. The hierarchical organization of folders and files can be represented as a tree structure. The root of the tree represents the main directory, with subsequent nodes representing subdirectories and files. This hierarchical arrangement allows for efficient navigation and organization of files, as well as the ability to define relationships and dependencies between different components.

Tree

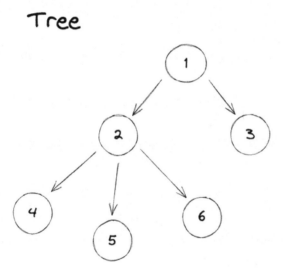

Another real-life application of trees can be found in decision-making processes. Decision trees are commonly used in fields such as artificial intelligence, machine learning, and data analysis. A decision tree represents a set of decisions and their possible outcomes, organized in a hierarchical manner. Each node in the tree represents a decision point, branching out to different paths based on the outcomes of the decisions. This structured representation helps in understanding complex decision-making processes and can aid in making informed choices.

Trees can be classified into various types based on their characteristics, such as binary trees, AVL trees, or B-trees. Each type has its own set of rules and properties, making it suitable for specific applications. For instance, binary trees restrict each node to have at most two children, making them efficient for searching and sorting operations.

Trees, with their hierarchical structure, offer a powerful way to organize and represent data. By understanding their real-life applications and analogies, you gain insights into how trees facilitate efficient file systems, decision-making processes, and more. As we continue our exploration of data structures and algorithms, remember the significance of trees and their ability to capture complex relationships and hierarchies in various domains.

Graphs: Modeling Relationships and Connections

In the realm of data structures, graphs provide a powerful framework for modeling relationships and connections between entities. Imagine a map with cities as nodes and roads as edges, where you can visualize how different locations are interconnected. This analogy helps us grasp the essence of graphs, a versatile and dynamic data structure with numerous real-life applications.

A graph consists of a set of nodes, also known as vertices, and a set of edges that connect these vertices. The edges represent relationships or connections between the vertices, forming a network-like structure. Graphs can be either directed, where the edges have a specific direction, or undirected, where the edges have no direction.

Graphs find applications in various domains. Consider social networks like Facebook or LinkedIn, where users are represented as nodes, and their connections are represented as edges. This interconnected structure allows users to establish relationships, communicate, and share information. Graph algorithms can be used to analyze these networks, identify influential users, or recommend connections based on common interests.

Another real-life example of graphs can be found in transportation networks. Think of an airline route map, where airports are represented as nodes, and flights between them are represented as edges. This graph structure enables efficient route planning, analysis of flight connections, and optimization of airline schedules. Graph algorithms can be used to find the shortest path between two destinations or determine the most optimal route considering factors like time, cost, or availability.

Graphs can be classified into various types, such as weighted graphs, bipartite graphs, or cyclic graphs, depending on their characteristics and properties. Each type serves different purposes and allows for specific analysis or optimization techniques.

Graphs provide a versatile and dynamic framework for modeling relationships and connections. By understanding their real-life applications and analogies, you gain insights into how graphs facilitate social networking, transportation planning, and more. As we continue our exploration of data structures and algorithms, remember the significance of graphs and their ability to capture intricate relationships and interconnections in diverse domains.

Graph

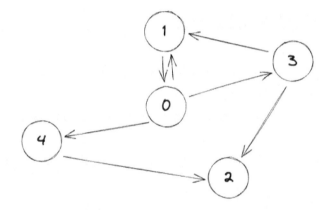

Graph Algorithms: Analyzing Relationships and Connectivity

In the realm of data structures and algorithms, graph algorithms play a vital role in analyzing relationships, connectivity, and optimizing operations within graph structures. Imagine you are planning a road trip and want to find the shortest route between multiple cities. This analogy helps us understand the importance of graph algorithms, which enable efficient traversal and analysis of interconnected networks.

Graph algorithms provide a set of techniques for solving various problems within graph structures. They help uncover valuable insights, identify patterns, and optimize operations in real-life scenarios. Let's explore some prominent graph algorithms and their practical applications.

Depth-First Search (DFS): DFS is a graph traversal algorithm that explores as far as possible along each branch before backtracking. It can be used to determine connectivity, detect cycles, and find paths within a graph. For example, DFS can be applied to explore web pages or social networks to discover connections and relationships among entities.

Breadth-First Search (BFS): BFS is another graph traversal algorithm that explores all the neighbors of a node before moving to the next level. It helps find the shortest path between two nodes and is widely used in network routing, social network analysis, and web crawling. BFS can be employed to determine the fewest number of connections required to reach a person on a social media platform.

Dijkstra's Algorithm: Dijkstra's algorithm is used to find the shortest path between two nodes in a weighted graph. It considers the weight or cost associated with each edge and selects the most optimal path. This algorithm is utilized in transportation planning, route optimization, and network routing to find the most efficient paths, minimizing travel time or costs.

Kruskal's Algorithm: Kruskal's algorithm is used to find the minimum spanning tree of a weighted graph. It helps identify the subset of edges that connect all the nodes with the minimum total weight. This algorithm is applied in network design, electrical distribution systems, and clustering analysis to determine the optimal connections and minimize overall costs.

These are just a few examples of graph algorithms among many others, including Prim's algorithm, Bellman-Ford algorithm, and Floyd-Warshall algorithm, each with its specific purpose and applications.

Graph algorithms provide powerful tools for analyzing relationships, connectivity, and optimizing operations within graph structures. By understanding their real-life applications and analogies, you gain insights into how these algorithms enable efficient web crawling, social network analysis, transportation planning, and more. As we continue our exploration of data structures and algorithms, remember the significance of graph algorithms and their ability to uncover valuable insights in diverse domains.

Sorting Algorithms: Organizing Data for Efficiency

In the realm of data structures and algorithms, sorting algorithms are essential tools for organizing data in a specific order. Imagine a librarian categorizing books on the shelves based on their titles or authors. This analogy helps us understand the significance of sorting algorithms, which enable efficient searching, analysis, and retrieval of data.

Sorting algorithms provide techniques to arrange elements in a specific order, such as ascending or descending, based on defined criteria. Let's explore some commonly used sorting algorithms and their practical applications.

Bubble Sort: Bubble sort is a simple and intuitive sorting algorithm that repeatedly compares adjacent elements and swaps them if they are in the wrong order. It continues iterating through the list until no more swaps are required. Although bubble sort is not the most efficient algorithm for large datasets, it serves as a fundamental concept for understanding sorting techniques.

Selection Sort: Selection sort works by repeatedly selecting the smallest element from the unsorted portion of the list and placing it in the correct position. This process is repeated until the entire list is sorted. While selection sort is straightforward to understand and implement, it is not efficient for large datasets due to its time complexity.

Insertion Sort: Insertion sort builds the final sorted array one element at a time by repeatedly inserting each element into its correct position within the sorted portion of the array. It is often used for small datasets or when the input is already partially sorted.

Merge Sort: Merge sort is a divide-and-conquer algorithm that divides the input list into smaller sublists, recursively sorts them, and then merges them to obtain the final sorted array. Merge sort has a time complexity of $O(n \log n)$ and is widely used for sorting large datasets efficiently.

Quick Sort: Quick sort is another divide-and-conquer algorithm that selects a pivot element, partitions the list into two sublists, and recursively sorts them. It has an average time complexity of $O(n \log n)$ and is known for its efficiency and practicality.

Sorting algorithms have diverse applications in various fields. For example, in the e-commerce industry, sorting algorithms are used to arrange products based on price, popularity, or customer reviews.

Searching Algorithms: Finding What You Need

In the realm of data structures and algorithms, searching algorithms are indispensable tools for finding specific elements within a collection of data. Imagine searching for a particular book in a vast library with thousands of books. This analogy helps us understand the significance of searching algorithms, which enable efficient retrieval of information from large datasets.

Searching algorithms provide techniques to locate a specific element within a dataset. Let's explore some commonly used searching algorithms and their practical applications.

Linear Search: Linear search is a simple and straightforward algorithm that sequentially checks each element in a list until the desired element is found or the entire list is traversed. While linear search is easy to implement, it is not the most efficient algorithm for large datasets.

Binary Search: Binary search is a divide-and-conquer algorithm that works on sorted lists. It repeatedly divides the search space in half and compares the middle element with the target value. By eliminating half of the search space at each step, binary search quickly converges to the desired element. It is highly efficient for large sorted datasets and is widely used in various applications.

Hashing: Hashing is a technique that uses hash functions to map keys to array indices, providing fast access to elements. Hashing is often used in conjunction with data structures like hash tables to enable efficient searching, insertion, and deletion operations. It finds applications in databases, caching systems, and information retrieval systems.

Tree-based Searching: Tree data structures such as binary search trees, AVL trees, and B-trees offer efficient searching capabilities. These structures allow for faster searching by organizing elements in a hierarchical manner. Tree-based searching is widely used in database systems, file systems, and search engines to enable efficient retrieval of information.

Searching algorithms have diverse applications in everyday life. For instance, in web search engines, searching algorithms enable users to find relevant information quickly from a vast amount of web pages. In GPS navigation systems, searching algorithms help locate addresses or points of interest efficiently.

Searching algorithms play a crucial role in finding specific elements within datasets, allowing for efficient information retrieval. By understanding their real-life applications and analogies, you gain insights into how these algorithms power web search engines, GPS navigation systems, and more. As we continue our exploration of data structures and algorithms, remember the significance of searching algorithms and their ability to quickly locate the information you need in diverse domains.

Hashing: Efficient Data Retrieval with Hash Tables

In the realm of data structures and algorithms, hashing is a powerful technique used for efficient data retrieval. Imagine a large library with thousands of books, each assigned a unique identification number and stored in a specific location. This analogy helps us understand the significance of hashing, which enables quick and direct access to stored information based on a unique key.

Hashing is a process that involves mapping data elements to specific positions in a data structure called a hash table. This mapping is done using a hash function, which takes the key as input and produces a hash value or index. Let's explore the concept of hashing and its practical applications.

Hash Functions: A hash function is a mathematical function that takes an input (such as a key) and produces a unique hash value. It should distribute the keys uniformly across the hash table to minimize collisions, where two keys produce the same hash value. Well-designed hash functions ensure efficient data retrieval and minimize the number of collisions.

Hash Tables: A hash table is a data structure that uses an array combined with hashing to store and retrieve data. Each element is stored at a specific index in the array, determined by its hash value. Hash tables provide fast access to elements by directly calculating the index using the hash function. They are widely used in various applications, including databases, caching systems, symbol tables, and spell checkers.

Collision Resolution: Collisions occur when two different keys produce the same hash value and need to be stored at the same index in the hash table. Various collision resolution techniques, such as chaining and open addressing, are used to handle collisions efficiently. These techniques ensure that all elements can be stored and retrieved correctly, even when collisions occur.

Real-life applications of hashing are abundant. For example, in database systems, hashing allows for efficient retrieval of records based on primary keys. Hashing is also used in password storage, where passwords are hashed and stored in a database for secure authentication without storing the actual passwords. Additionally, hashing plays a vital role in cryptographic algorithms to ensure data integrity and security.

4

Analyzing Algorithm Efficiency

Understanding Algorithm Analysis

In the world of algorithms, understanding and analyzing their efficiency is of paramount importance. Imagine being tasked with solving a complex problem, but not knowing whether your solution will execute in a reasonable amount of time or use excessive memory. This is where algorithm analysis comes into play, helping us evaluate and compare the efficiency of different algorithms.

Algorithm analysis involves studying the behavior of algorithms and quantifying their performance characteristics. It enables us to determine how an algorithm's execution time and memory usage grow as the input size increases. By analyzing algorithms, we can make informed decisions about which ones to use for specific tasks and identify opportunities for optimization.

Why is algorithm analysis crucial? Consider a real-life scenario: You're designing a route optimization algorithm for a delivery company. The efficiency of your algorithm directly impacts the time taken for deliveries, fuel consumption, and customer satisfaction. Analyzing the algorithm's efficiency ensures that it can handle a growing number of delivery locations while maintaining optimal performance.

Algorithm analysis also helps identify inefficiencies that can be improved upon. For instance, the bubble sort algorithm is simple to understand and implement, but it has poor time complexity for large datasets. By analyzing its efficiency, we can discover more efficient sorting algorithms like quicksort or merge sort.

To perform algorithm analysis, we consider factors such as time complexity, space complexity, and the impact of input size on algorithm performance. Time complexity measures how the algorithm's execution time grows with input size, while space complexity evaluates its memory usage. These analyses enable us to compare algorithms and make informed choices based on the requirements of the problem at hand.

Real-life stories demonstrate the significance of algorithm analysis. For example, the Google search engine handles billions of queries daily, and analyzing the efficiency of its search algorithms ensures fast and accurate results. The Netflix recommendation system relies on analyzing the efficiency of recommendation algorithms to provide personalized content to millions of users.

Algorithm analysis empowers us to make informed decisions when choosing algorithms for a wide range of applications. By understanding the concepts and techniques of algorithm analysis, you can confidently evaluate and compare the efficiency of algorithms, leading to optimized solutions in problem-solving. In the following sections, we will delve deeper into complexity theory and asymptotic notations, providing you with powerful tools to measure and compare algorithm efficiency.

Complexity Theory: Foundations of Efficiency

In the world of algorithms, complexity theory forms the bedrock for understanding and evaluating algorithm efficiency. It provides us with a theoretical framework to analyze and classify the performance characteristics of algorithms. By studying complexity theory, we gain valuable insights into how algorithms behave and how their efficiency scales with input size.

Complexity theory focuses on two fundamental aspects: time complexity and space complexity. Time complexity refers to how the running time of an algorithm grows as the input size increases. Space complexity, on the other hand, pertains to the amount of memory an algorithm requires to solve a problem based on the input size.

To understand the essence of complexity theory, let's delve into a real-life scenario: social networking platforms. Facebook, with over 2.8 billion monthly active users, faces the challenge of efficiently displaying content on users' newsfeeds. Complexity theory helps in analyzing and optimizing algorithms responsible for determining which posts to show, taking into account factors such as user preferences, friendship connections, and post relevance. By understanding the time and space complexities of these algorithms, Facebook can ensure a seamless user experience even with a massive user base.

One of the key concepts in complexity theory is the notion of scalability. Scalability refers to an algorithm's ability to handle increasing input sizes without a significant increase in resources or time. An algorithm that exhibits good scalability is capable of solving larger problems efficiently, which is essential in real-world scenarios where data sizes and user demands can grow exponentially.

In addition to scalability, complexity theory introduces the concept of upper and lower bounds. The upper bound, often expressed using Big O notation, represents the worst-case scenario or an upper limit on the algorithm's running time or memory usage. The lower bound, represented by Omega notation, provides insights into the best-case scenario or a lower limit on the algorithm's performance. Theta notation, used to express tight bounds, characterizes both the upper and lower limits of an algorithm's efficiency.

Understanding the foundations of complexity theory equips us with the necessary tools to evaluate and compare algorithm efficiency. By analyzing the time and space complexities of different algorithms, we can make informed decisions about which algorithm to use based on the problem at hand. Complexity theory empowers us to optimize our solutions, ensuring they are efficient, scalable, and capable of handling real-world demands.

Asymptotic Notation: Big O, Omega, and Theta

In the world of algorithm analysis, expressing and comparing the efficiency of algorithms is crucial. To achieve this, we rely on asymptotic notations, such as Big O, Omega, and Theta. These notations provide a powerful and concise way to describe the growth rates of algorithms and understand their upper and lower bounds.

Imagine you're developing a navigation app that provides real-time traffic information. The efficiency of your route planning algorithm directly impacts the app's responsiveness and accuracy. By employing asymptotic notations, you can precisely analyze the algorithm's performance and choose the most efficient solution.

Let's start with Big O notation, denoted as $O(f(n))$. It represents the upper bound of an algorithm's time complexity. In simpler terms, it describes how an algorithm's running time grows relative to the input size. For example, if an algorithm has a time complexity of $O(n^2)$, it means that its running time grows quadratically as the input size increases.

On the other hand, Omega notation (Ω) provides the lower bound of an algorithm's time complexity. It signifies the best-case scenario or the lower limit of the algorithm's performance. Omega notation helps us understand the inherent efficiency of an algorithm. For instance, if an algorithm has a time complexity of $\Omega(n)$, it means that its running time must grow at least linearly with the input size.

Theta notation (Θ) combines both the upper and lower bounds, providing a tight characterization of an algorithm's time complexity. It represents a range in which an algorithm's performance falls. For example, if an algorithm has a time complexity of $\Theta(n)$, it means that its running time grows linearly with the input size, without exceeding or falling below this growth rate.

Asymptotic notations allow us to compare algorithms and assess their efficiency. For instance, suppose we have two sorting algorithms, one with a time complexity of $O(n^2)$ and another with $O(n \log n)$. By comparing the notations, we can conclude that the latter algorithm is more efficient for larger input sizes.

Applying asymptotic notations to real-life scenarios is vital for making informed decisions. Consider a large-scale e-commerce platform like Amazon, where thousands of products are listed and searched for every second. By analyzing and comparing the efficiency of search algorithms using asymptotic notations, Amazon can ensure that product searches are executed quickly and deliver relevant results to customers.

Algorithmic Analysis Techniques

In addition to asymptotic notations, there are several techniques and strategies for analyzing the efficiency of algorithms. These techniques help us gain deeper insights into how algorithms perform and allow us to make informed decisions when designing or optimizing solutions. In this section, we will explore some of these techniques, including time complexity analysis, space complexity analysis, and pseudo code examples.

Time Complexity Analysis

Time complexity analysis involves determining how the running time of an algorithm increases with the size of the input. It helps us understand the scalability and efficiency of algorithms in handling larger problem instances. There are various approaches to analyze time complexity, such as counting the number of iterations, measuring the number of basic operations, or using recurrence relations. Pseudo code examples can assist in illustrating the step-by-step execution of an algorithm and help analyze its time complexity.

For instance, let's consider a pseudo code example of the classic bubble sort algorithm, which sorts an array in ascending order:

```
function bubbleSort(arr: array):
  n = length(arr)
  for i from 0 to n-1
    for j from 0 to n-i-1
      if arr[j] > arr[j+1]
        swap(arr[j], arr[j+1])
```

In the pseudo code above, we can observe that there are two nested loops, indicating that the algorithm iterates over the array multiple times. By analyzing the pseudo code and counting the iterations, we can determine that the time complexity of bubble sort is $O(n^2)$.

Space Complexity Analysis:
While time complexity focuses on the running time of an algorithm, space complexity analysis examines the amount of memory an algorithm requires to solve a problem. It helps us understand how the memory usage grows as the input size increases. Analyzing space complexity is essential, especially when working with limited memory resources or optimizing memory consumption. Similar to time complexity analysis, pseudo code examples can be used to analyze space complexity by tracking the memory used by variables, arrays, or data structures throughout the algorithm's execution.

Google's PageRank Algorithm

A fascinating real-life example of algorithmic analysis is Google's PageRank algorithm. PageRank revolutionized web search by ranking web pages based on their importance and relevance. The algorithm's efficiency played a critical role in handling the vast amount of web pages and providing users with accurate search results. Google's engineers employed rigorous algorithmic analysis techniques to optimize the PageRank algorithm's running time and memory usage, ensuring fast and efficient search results even for billions of web pages.

By applying these analysis techniques, engineers were able to refine the algorithm and make it scalable for the exponential growth of the web. It is a testament to the significance of algorithmic analysis in real-world applications.

Algorithmic Paradigms and Optimization Techniques

In the quest for efficient algorithms, various algorithmic paradigms and optimization techniques have been developed to tackle different problem scenarios. These approaches offer innovative strategies for solving complex problems and optimizing algorithm performance. In this section, we will explore some of these paradigms and techniques, including divide and conquer, greedy algorithms, and dynamic programming.

Divide and Conquer

Divide and conquer is a powerful algorithmic paradigm that involves breaking down a problem into smaller, more manageable subproblems, solving them independently, and then combining the solutions to obtain the final result. This approach is particularly useful for solving problems that can be divided into smaller, similar subproblems. By reducing the problem size and leveraging parallelism, divide and conquer algorithms can achieve significant performance improvements.

A classic example of the divide and conquer paradigm is the merge sort algorithm. Let's take a look at the pseudo code example:

```
function mergeSort(arr: array):
   if length(arr) <= 1
      return arr
   mid = length(arr) / 2
   left = mergeSort(arr[0:mid])
   right = mergeSort(arr[mid:length(arr)])
   return merge(left, right)

function merge(left: array, right: array):
   result = []
   while length(left) > 0 and length(right) > 0
      if left[0] <= right[0]
         append left[0] to result
         remove left[0]
      else
         append right[0] to result
         remove right[0]
   append remaining elements of left to result
   append remaining elements of right to result
   return result
```

In the pseudo code above, the merge sort algorithm employs divide and conquer by recursively splitting the input array into smaller halves until each subarray contains only one element. It then merges the sorted subarrays to obtain the final sorted array. The time complexity of merge sort is O(n log n), making it an efficient sorting algorithm.

Greedy Algorithms

Greedy algorithms make locally optimal choices at each step with the hope of finding a global optimum. These algorithms are useful when there is a need to make a series of decisions and each decision affects subsequent steps. Greedy algorithms focus on immediate gains without considering future consequences. While they may not always produce the best solution globally, they often provide acceptable solutions quickly.

A real-life example of a greedy algorithm is the activity selection problem. Imagine you have a set of activities with start and finish times, and you want to select the maximum number of non-overlapping activities. The greedy approach would be to sort the activities based on their finish times and greedily select the activities with the earliest finish times that do not overlap. This approach guarantees an optimal solution.

Dynamic Programming

Dynamic programming is a technique that solves complex problems by breaking them down into overlapping subproblems and solving each subproblem only once, storing the solutions in a table for future use. It is particularly useful for problems that exhibit optimal substructure, meaning that the optimal solution to the problem can be constructed from optimal solutions to its subproblems.

One classic example of dynamic programming is the Fibonacci sequence. The Fibonacci numbers can be calculated using a dynamic programming approach, as shown in the pseudo code example:

```
function fibonacci(n):
    if n <= 1
        return n
    memo = array of size n+1
    memo[0] = 0
    memo[1] = 1
    for i from 2 to n
        memo[i] = memo[i-1] + memo[i-2]
    return memo[n]
```

In the pseudo code above, dynamic programming is employed by storing the previously calculated Fibonacci numbers in the memo array, eliminating redundant calculations. This significantly improves the efficiency of computing Fibonacci numbers.

By utilizing algorithmic paradigms such as divide and conquer, greedy algorithms, and dynamic programming, we can design efficient solutions to complex problems. These techniques offer valuable strategies for optimizing algorithm performance and finding solutions that meet the requirements of real-world scenarios. In the next sections, we will explore more advanced topics in algorithmic analysis and expand our toolkit for problem-solving.

Optimization Techniques and Heuristics

In addition to algorithmic paradigms, there are various optimization techniques and heuristics that can further enhance the efficiency and effectiveness of algorithms. These approaches provide strategies for finding approximate solutions, improving performance, and handling complex problem domains. In this section, we will explore some of these optimization techniques and heuristics, including approximation algorithms, metaheuristics, and local search.

Approximation Algorithms

Approximation algorithms are designed to find near-optimal solutions for computationally challenging problems. These algorithms sacrifice optimality for efficiency by providing solutions that are guaranteed to be close to the optimal solution. While they may not always provide the exact optimal solution, they offer practical solutions within a reasonable time frame. Approximation algorithms are commonly used in NP-hard problems, where finding an exact optimal solution is infeasible.

A well-known example of an approximation algorithm is the Traveling Salesperson Problem (TSP). The TSP involves finding the shortest possible route that visits a set of cities and returns to the starting city. The problem is known to be NP-hard, making it computationally intensive to find the exact optimal solution. However, there exist approximation algorithms that can find a solution within a certain factor of the optimal solution, enabling efficient route planning for practical scenarios.

Metaheuristics
Metaheuristics are high-level optimization techniques that guide the search for solutions in large solution spaces. They are general-purpose algorithms that can be applied to various problems and do not guarantee finding the optimal solution. Instead, they focus on exploring the solution space efficiently and providing good-quality solutions within a reasonable time. Metaheuristics often incorporate concepts from nature-inspired algorithms, such as genetic algorithms, simulated annealing, and particle swarm optimization.

Consider the Knapsack Problem, where we have a set of items with different weights and values, and we need to

Local Search

Local search is an optimization technique that iteratively improves a solution by making incremental modifications to it. It starts with an initial solution and explores the neighborhood of solutions by applying local modifications. The goal is to gradually move towards better solutions until an optimal or satisfactory solution is reached.

An example of a local search algorithm is the Hill Climbing algorithm. It starts with an initial solution and makes small changes, evaluating if each change leads to an improvement. If an improvement is found, the modified solution becomes the new starting point for the next iteration. The algorithm continues until no further improvements can be made. While local search algorithms may not guarantee finding the global optimum, they can efficiently find good solutions in various optimization problems.

Google Maps and Optimization Techniques

Google Maps is a prime example of how optimization techniques can be applied to real-life scenarios. By leveraging approximation algorithms, metaheuristics, and local search techniques, Google Maps can efficiently calculate the shortest routes, estimate travel times, and provide real-time traffic updates. These optimization techniques enable Google Maps to handle the complexity of millions of routes and provide users with optimal directions, even in dynamic traffic conditions.

Advanced Algorithmic Techniques

In the realm of algorithm design, there are advanced techniques that offer sophisticated approaches to solving complex problems efficiently. These techniques leverage specialized data structures, optimization strategies, and algorithmic concepts to address specific challenges. In this section, we will explore some of these advanced algorithmic techniques, including dynamic programming, backtracking, and randomized algorithms.

Dynamic Programming

Dynamic programming, which we briefly touched upon earlier, is a powerful technique for solving optimization problems by breaking them down into overlapping subproblems and solving each subproblem only once. It relies on storing the solutions to subproblems in a table or memoization array for efficient lookup.

One classic example of dynamic programming is the Longest Common Subsequence (LCS) problem. Given two sequences, the LCS problem involves finding the longest subsequence that is common to both sequences. Dynamic programming can be used to solve this problem by building a memoization table and iteratively filling it based on the recurrence relation.

Consider the following pseudo code example for finding the length of the LCS:

```
function LCSLength(X: string, Y: string):
m = length(X)
n = length(Y)
L = array[m+1][n+1]
for i from 0 to m
  for j from 0 to n
    if i = 0 or j = 0
      L[i][j] = 0
    else if X[i-1] = Y[j-1]
      L[i][j] = L[i-1][j-1] + 1
    else
      L[i][j] = max(L[i-1][j], L[i][j-1])
return L[m][n]
```

In the pseudo code above, the dynamic programming approach computes the length of the LCS by populating the memoization table `L`. The time complexity of this algorithm is O(mn), where m and n are the lengths of the input sequences.

Backtracking
Backtracking is a systematic approach for finding solutions by incrementally building candidates and exploring different possibilities. It is particularly useful for solving problems with a large search space or when an exhaustive search is required. Backtracking algorithms employ a depth-first search strategy and intelligently backtrack

when they encounter partial solutions that cannot be extended to a valid solution.

The N-Queens problem is a classic example that can be solved using backtracking. In this problem, the task is to place N queens on an N×N chessboard such that no two queens threaten each other. Backtracking algorithms can efficiently explore the solution space by placing queens on the board one by one, checking for conflicts at each step, and backtracking when conflicts arise.

Randomized Algorithms

Randomized algorithms utilize randomness as an integral part of their design to improve efficiency or overcome certain problem constraints. By introducing randomization, these algorithms can achieve faster average-case performance or find solutions that are otherwise difficult to obtain deterministically.

One example of a randomized algorithm is the QuickSort algorithm. QuickSort employs a random pivot selection strategy, which partitions the input array based on the pivot element. This randomization reduces the likelihood of worst-case behavior and improves the average-case time complexity of the algorithm to $O(n \log n)$.

Simulated Annealing and Optimization

Simulated annealing is a popular optimization technique inspired by the physical process of annealing in metallurgy. It has been successfully applied to various real-life optimization problems, such as the traveling salesperson problem, resource allocation, and network optimization. Simulated annealing uses randomization and iterative improvement to search for near-optimal solutions in complex problem spaces. By gradually decreasing the temperature parameter, it escapes local optima and explores the solution space more effectively.

Algorithmic Optimization and Trade-offs

When designing algorithms, it is crucial to consider not only their correctness and efficiency but also the trade-offs associated with different approaches. Algorithmic optimization involves finding the right balance between various factors such as time complexity, space complexity, simplicity, and maintainability. In this section, we will explore the concept of algorithmic optimization and discuss some common trade-offs that arise during the algorithm design process.

Time Complexity vs. Space Complexity

One of the primary trade-offs in algorithm design is between time complexity and space complexity. Improving the time complexity of an algorithm may require using additional memory or data structures, which can increase the space complexity. Conversely, optimizing space usage may lead to more computationally intensive operations and potentially slower execution.

Consider the example of sorting algorithms. QuickSort has an average-case time complexity of $O(n \log n)$ but requires additional space for recursive function calls, resulting in higher space complexity. On the other hand, algorithms like Insertion Sort or Selection Sort have lower space complexity but higher time complexity.

The choice between time complexity and space complexity depends on the specific requirements of the problem at hand. If memory usage is a concern, sacrificing some time efficiency for reduced space usage may be preferable. Conversely, if execution time is critical, optimizing for time complexity might take precedence.

Algorithmic Techniques and Complexity

Different algorithmic techniques have varying impacts on the complexity of the problem. Some techniques, such as greedy algorithms or dynamic programming, can lead to more efficient solutions, but they may also introduce additional complexity in terms of implementation and analysis.

For example, the Knapsack Problem can be solved using both greedy and dynamic programming approaches. A greedy algorithm for the Knapsack Problem selects items based on their individual value-to-weight ratios, making locally optimal choices at each step. This approach has a time complexity of O(n log n) but does not guarantee an optimal solution in all cases.

In contrast, dynamic programming can solve the Knapsack Problem optimally but introduces additional complexity in terms of implementing the memoization table and defining the recurrence relation. The dynamic programming solution has a time complexity of $O(nW)$, where n is the number of items and W is the maximum weight that the knapsack can hold.

Choosing the appropriate algorithmic technique depends on the problem requirements and the balance between time complexity, optimality, and simplicity.

Domain-Specific Optimization

In some cases, algorithmic optimization involves considering domain-specific characteristics and constraints. By exploiting specific properties of the problem domain, we can develop specialized algorithms that outperform generic approaches.

For instance, in image compression algorithms like JPEG, specific optimizations take advantage of properties such as frequency domain representation, human visual perception, and color space conversions. These optimizations result in more efficient compression and decompression algorithms tailored for image data.

Similarly, graph algorithms often have optimizations based on graph properties such as sparsity, connectivity, or planarity. By considering these domain-specific characteristics, we can design algorithms that leverage the structure of the problem to improve efficiency.

Optimization in Network Routing

Optimization plays a critical role in network routing, where the goal is to find the most efficient paths for data transmission. In large-scale networks, such as the Internet, efficient routing is crucial for minimizing delays, avoiding congestion, and maximizing network throughput.

One example of an optimization technique used in network routing is the Dijkstra's algorithm. It finds the shortest path between nodes in a graph by iteratively selecting the node with the lowest distance. Dijkstra's algorithm optimizes for path length but requires additional memory to store distances and paths.

Another optimization technique used in network routing is the Bellman-Ford algorithm, which handles negative edge weights and is widely used in routing protocols like the Border Gateway Protocol (BGP). The Bellman-Ford algorithm optimizes for robustness and reliability but has a higher time complexity compared to Dijkstra's algorithm.

These real-life examples demonstrate how algorithmic optimization plays a crucial role in network routing, where finding the most efficient paths is essential for smooth and reliable data transmission.

By considering the trade-offs between time complexity, space complexity, algorithmic techniques, and domain-specific optimizations, algorithm designers can make informed decisions to achieve the most efficient and effective solutions for a given problem.

5

Recursion and Backtracking

Understanding Recursion

Recursion is a powerful and elegant concept in computer science that allows us to solve complex problems by breaking them down into simpler subproblems. It involves defining a function that calls itself to solve a smaller version of the original problem, eventually leading to the base case where the recursion stops. In this section, we will delve into the intricacies of recursion, understand its fundamental concepts, and explore its real-life applications.

Recursion can be seen as a process where a problem is divided into smaller subproblems, and each subproblem is solved by invoking the same function. This recursive approach allows us to tackle complex problems by reducing them to simpler instances. By breaking down the problem into smaller parts, we can solve each part independently and combine the results to obtain the final solution.

The Recursive Function

A recursive function consists of two essential components: the base case and the recursive case. The base case defines the simplest form of the problem that can be solved directly without further recursion. It acts as the terminating condition for the recursion. The recursive case defines how the function calls itself to solve a smaller version of the problem. This recursive call continues until the base case is reached.

Recursion finds applications in various domains, from mathematics to computer science and beyond. Let's explore a real-life example to illustrate the concept of recursion:

Real-life Story: Fractals and the Mandelbrot Set
One remarkable application of recursion is the generation of fractals, which are intricate and self-repeating geometric patterns. The Mandelbrot Set, discovered by mathematician Benoit Mandelbrot, is a famous example of a fractal.

The Mandelbrot Set is defined by a simple mathematical formula, but its complexity and beauty emerge when visualized. To generate the Mandelbrot Set, one must iterate through each point on a complex plane and determine whether it belongs to the set or not. The iterative process involves applying a recursive formula for each point, where the result of each iteration is fed back into the next.

The recursive nature of the formula allows for the creation of intricate and infinitely detailed patterns within the Mandelbrot Set. This example demonstrates how recursion can be used to generate complex and visually captivating structures.

Pseudo Code Example

To further illustrate the concept of recursion, let's consider a classic example: calculating the factorial of a number.

```
function factorial(n):
    if n == 0:      // Base case: factorial of 0 is 1
        return 1
    else:           // Recursive case: multiply n by factorial(n-1)
        return n * factorial(n-1)
```

In this pseudo code, the factorial function is defined recursively. The base case is when n equals 0, where the factorial is defined as 1. In the recursive case, the function multiplies n by the factorial of (n-1). This process continues until the base case is reached.

By understanding the fundamental concepts of recursion, we unlock a powerful problem-solving tool. Recursion allows us to break down complex problems into manageable pieces and solve them in an elegant and efficient manner. However, it is essential to consider the trade-offs of recursion, such as potential stack overflow for deeply recursive algorithms or the need for extra memory.

Solving Problems with Recursion

Recursion provides a powerful approach to problem-solving, allowing us to break down complex problems into simpler subproblems. In this section, we will explore how recursion can be used to solve a variety of problems effectively. We will examine the process of identifying base cases and recursive cases, and we will discuss recursive algorithms for common problems. Let's dive into the world of problem-solving with recursion.

Recursive Problem-Solving Strategies

When approaching a problem using recursion, it is essential to identify the base case and the recursive case. The base case represents the simplest form of the problem that can be solved directly. It acts as the terminating condition for the recursion. The recursive case defines how the problem is broken down into smaller subproblems and how the function calls itself to solve them. By recursively solving the subproblems and combining their results, we can arrive at the solution to the original problem.

Identifying Base Cases and Recursive Cases
To effectively solve a problem with recursion, we need to identify the base case and recursive case(s). The base case represents the smallest possible instance of the problem that can be solved directly. It helps us determine when to stop the recursion. The recursive case defines how the problem is divided into smaller subproblems that are closer to the base case. By continually applying the recursive case, we move closer to the base case until it is reached, allowing the recursion to terminate.

Recursive Algorithms for Common Problems
Recursive algorithms are often used to solve various problems across different domains. Let's explore some common examples:

a) Factorial:
Calculating the factorial of a non-negative integer is a classic example of a recursive problem. The factorial of a number is defined as the product of all positive integers up to and including that number. The recursive algorithm for calculating the factorial can be expressed as follows:

terminating condition for the recursion. The recursive case defines how the problem is broken down into smaller subproblems and how the function calls itself to solve them. By recursively solving the subproblems and combining their results, we can arrive at the solution to the original problem.

Identifying Base Cases and Recursive Cases
To effectively solve a problem with recursion, we need to identify the base case and recursive case(s). The base case represents the smallest possible instance of the problem that can be solved directly. It helps us determine when to stop the recursion. The recursive case defines how the problem is divided into smaller subproblems that are closer to the base case. By continually applying the recursive case, we move closer to the base case until it is reached, allowing the recursion to terminate.

Recursive Algorithms for Common Problems
Recursive algorithms are often used to solve various problems across different domains. Let's explore some common examples:

a) Factorial:
Calculating the factorial of a non-negative integer is a classic example of a recursive problem. The factorial of a number is defined as the product of all positive integers up to and including that number. The recursive algorithm for calculating the factorial can be expressed as follows:

function factorial(n):
  if n == 0:   // Base case: factorial of 0 is 1
    return 1
  else: // Recursive case: multiply n by factorial(n-1)
    return n * factorial(n-1)

b) Fibonacci Sequence:

The Fibonacci sequence is a series of numbers in which each number is the sum of the two preceding ones. The recursive algorithm for generating the Fibonacci sequence can be expressed as follows:

function fibonacci(n):
  if n <= 1:   // Base case: Fibonacci of 0 and 1 is the number itself
    return n
  else: // Recursive case: sum of the two preceding Fibonacci numbers
    return fibonacci(n-1) + fibonacci(n-2)

Real-life Example: Maze Solving
Recursion finds practical applications in solving mazes. Imagine you are trapped in a maze and need to find your way out. By applying a recursive algorithm, you can explore different paths until you reach the exit.

Real-life Story: The Maze Escape
Consider the story of Alice, a young adventurer who finds herself trapped in an ancient labyrinth. The labyrinth is a complex network of interconnected passages, some leading to dead ends and others leading to the exit.

Alice decides to apply recursion to navigate the maze. She starts at the entrance and explores each passage recursively. At each intersection, she chooses a path, marks it, and follows it until she reaches either a dead end or the exit. If she reaches a dead end, she backtracks and tries a different path, repeating the process until she successfully finds the exit.

By using recursion, Alice effectively explores the entire maze and discovers the path to freedom. This real-life example illustrates the power of recursion in solving complex problems.

By understanding the strategies for recursive problem-solving, identifying base and recursive cases, and exploring recursive algorithms, we gain a deeper understanding of how recursion can be applied to solve a wide range of problems effectively. In the next section, we will explore backtracking, another problem-solving technique that complements recursion and expands our problem-solving toolkit.

Exploring Backtracking

Backtracking is a powerful problem-solving technique that allows us to systematically search through all possible solutions to a problem. It is especially useful when we need to find one or more solutions among a large set of possibilities. In this section, we will delve into the concept of backtracking, understand its principles, and explore its applications in solving complex problems.

Principles of Backtracking

Backtracking is a systematic approach that involves exploring all possible solutions by incrementally building a solution and undoing the choices that lead to a dead end. It follows a depth-first search strategy, exploring a path until it is either solved or determined to be unsolvable, and then backtracking to explore other paths. The key components of a backtracking algorithm are:

a) Decision Space: It represents the set of choices or decisions we can make at each step of the problem-solving process. Each decision leads to a new state.

b) Constraints: Constraints define the conditions that must be satisfied for a solution to be valid. They help in pruning the search space and avoiding unnecessary exploration.

c) Pruning: Pruning involves early termination of a path if it violates any constraints or leads to a dead end. It helps reduce the search space and improve the efficiency of the algorithm.

Pseudocode Example: N-Queens Problem
One classic example that demonstrates the power of backtracking is the N-Queens problem. The problem involves placing N queens on an N×N chessboard in such a way that no two queens threaten each other. Let's take a look at the pseudocode for solving the N-Queens problem using backtracking:

```
function solveNQueens(board, row):
  if row == N:
    // Base case: All queens have been placed successfully
    printSolution(board)
    return

  for col in range(N):
    if isSafe(board, row, col):
      // Place the queen and move to the next row
      board[row][col] = 'Q'
      solveNQueens(board, row + 1)
      // Backtrack by removing the queen
      board[row][col] = '.'

function isSafe(board, row, col):
  // Check if placing a queen at the given position is safe
  // ...
```

In this pseudocode, we start with an empty chessboard and recursively place queens in each row. We check if the placement is safe by verifying that no other queen threatens the current position. If a safe placement is found, we move to the next row and repeat the process. If a solution is found, it is printed, and then we backtrack by removing the queen and exploring other possibilities.

Sudoku Solver
Another real-life application of backtracking is solving Sudoku puzzles. Sudoku is a popular number puzzle that requires filling a 9×9 grid with digits from 1 to 9, following certain constraints. Backtracking can be used to systematically explore different number placements until a valid solution is found.

The Sudoku Challenge
Imagine Sarah, an avid puzzle enthusiast, comes across a particularly challenging Sudoku puzzle. Determined to solve it, she decides to apply a backtracking algorithm.

Sarah starts by filling in the given numbers and then iteratively tries different number placements for each empty cell. She checks the constraints of the puzzle, making sure that no row, column, or 3×3 subgrid contains duplicate numbers. If a placement violates any constraints, she backtracks and explores a different possibility. Sarah continues this process until she finds a valid solution or exhausts all possibilities.

By utilizing backtracking, Sarah successfully solves the Sudoku puzzle, showcasing the power of this technique in solving complex problems.

By understanding the principles of back tracking and exploring its applications, we equip ourselves with a valuable problem-solving tool. In the next section, we will delve further into the challenges and strategies involved in implementing backtracking algorithms.

Memoization in Recursion

n this section, we will explore the concept of memoization and how it can be used to optimize recursive algorithms. Memoization is a powerful technique that allows us to store and reuse previously computed results, eliminating redundant computations and significantly improving the efficiency of recursive algorithms.

Memoization involves caching the results of expensive function calls and retrieving those results when the same inputs occur again. By storing the computed results in a data structure such as a hash table, we can avoid redundant computations and retrieve the precomputed results in constant time when needed.

Applying Memoization in Recursive Algorithms

Recursive algorithms often exhibit overlapping subproblems, meaning that the same subproblem is solved multiple times during the recursion. Memoization can be applied in such scenarios to avoid redundant computations by storing the results of previously solved subproblems.

Pseudocode Example: Fibonacci Sequence with Memoization

To illustrate the concept of memoization, let's consider the Fibonacci sequence, a classic example of a recursive algorithm. Here's an optimized version of the Fibonacci algorithm that uses memoization:

```
memo = {}

function fibonacci(n):
    if n in memo:
        return memo[n]

    if n <= 1:
        result = n
    else:
        result = fibonacci(n-1) + fibonacci(n-2)

    memo[n] = result
    return result
```

In this pseudocode, the `memo` dictionary is used to store the results of previously computed Fibonacci numbers. Before computing a Fibonacci number, we check if it is already present in the `memo`. If it is, we retrieve the result directly, avoiding redundant computations. Otherwise, we calculate the Fibonacci number recursively, store it in the `memo`, and return the result.

Advanced Backtracking Techniques

Pruning Techniques

One of the main challenges in backtracking is the potentially large search space. As the size of the problem increases, the number of possible solutions grows exponentially. Pruning techniques help us reduce unnecessary exploration by eliminating portions of the search space that are guaranteed to be invalid.

a) Constraint Propagation

Constraint propagation involves using problem-specific constraints to narrow down the search space. By enforcing these constraints during the search, we can eliminate large portions of the decision space. This technique is often used in constraint satisfaction problems such as Sudoku, where the placement of one number in a cell affects the constraints for neighboring cells.

b) Forward Checking

Forward checking is a technique where we keep track of

the remaining possible choices for each decision variable. When a decision is made, we update the list of available choices for other variables accordingly. If a variable has no available choices, we can prune that branch of the search space. This technique helps us detect potential dead ends early on.

Pseudocode Example: Subset Sum Problem

Let's consider the Subset Sum problem as an example to demonstrate the advanced backtracking techniques. Given a set of positive integers and a target sum, the problem asks whether there is a subset of the integers that sums up to the target. Here's the pseudocode for solving the Subset Sum problem using backtracking with pruning techniques:

```
function subsetSum(set, target):
   if target == 0:
      // Base case: Subset with the target sum is found
      return true
   if target < 0 or set is empty:
      // Base case: Subset with the target sum is not possible
      return false

   // Choose the first element and explore
   if subsetSum(set[1:], target - set[0]):
      // Backtrack if the subset is found
      return true

   // Exclude the first element and explore
   if subsetSum(set[1:], target):
      // Backtrack if the subset is found
      return true

   // No subset found
   return false
```

In this pseudocode, we recursively explore two possibilities at each step: including or excluding the current element. By using pruning techniques like checking the target sum and the empty set condition, we avoid unnecessary exploration and improve the efficiency of the algorithm.

6

Parallel and Distributed Algorithms

Parallel and distributed computing has revolutionized the way we approach problem-solving and opened doors to unprecedented scalability. Picture a team of individuals collaborating on a massive puzzle – each working on their piece independently but contributing to the overall solution. Similarly, parallel algorithms leverage multiple processors or computing nodes to divide and conquer problems, bringing dramatic speed-ups.

One notable example of parallelism's impact is the Folding@home project. Started in 2000, this distributed computing initiative utilizes the idle processing power of millions of volunteers' computers worldwide to simulate protein folding, aiding scientific research in areas such as understanding diseases and drug development. By harnessing the collective power of parallel processing, Folding@home has made remarkable strides in advancing medical knowledge and potential treatments.

Parallel algorithm paradigms, such as task parallelism and data parallelism, play a crucial role in designing efficient solutions. Task parallelism involves dividing a problem into smaller tasks that can be executed concurrently. A classic example is parallel sorting algorithms like Merge Sort, where different parts of the input array are sorted simultaneously. Data parallelism, on the other hand, focuses on dividing the input data into subsets that are processed independently. Graphics processing units (GPUs) excel in data parallelism, enabling fast computations for tasks like image rendering and machine learning.

In 2019, researchers at Stanford University leveraged parallel computing to make groundbreaking progress in gravitational wave astronomy. By parallelizing their algorithms and utilizing distributed computing resources, they successfully detected the collision of two neutron stars, a major milestone in our understanding of the universe. This achievement showcased the immense power of parallel and distributed algorithms in unlocking hidden secrets of the cosmos.

By embracing parallelism, we tap into a realm of limitless possibilities. From accelerating scientific breakthroughs to optimizing complex simulations and data analysis, parallel and distributed computing continues to shape our world. In the upcoming chapters, we will delve deeper into the intricacies of parallel algorithm design, exploring practical applications and emerging trends that push the boundaries of what is possible in the realm of computing. Get ready to witness the true potential of the algorithmic mindset unleashed through parallel and distributed algorithms.

Designing Parallel Algorithms

Designing algorithms that can be executed in parallel requires a deep understanding of the problem at hand and the ability to identify opportunities for parallelism. Let's dive into some techniques and approaches that will help us leverage parallelism effectively:

Task Parallelism: Task parallelism involves breaking down a problem into smaller tasks that can be executed concurrently. Each task operates on a different portion of the problem, allowing multiple processors or computing nodes to work simultaneously. One classic example is the MapReduce framework, which revolutionized big data processing. MapReduce divides a large dataset into smaller chunks and processes them in parallel, greatly reducing the time required for data analysis.

Google's implementation of the MapReduce framework transformed the landscape of big data analytics. By leveraging the power of parallelism, Google was able to process vast amounts of data in a highly efficient and scalable manner. This breakthrough paved the way for technologies like Apache Hadoop, enabling organizations worldwide to tackle big data challenges with ease.

Data Parallelism: Data parallelism involves dividing the input data into subsets and processing them independently. Each subset is processed by a separate processor or computing node, and the results are combined to obtain the final solution. This approach is particularly effective in tasks that involve performing the same operations on different portions of the data simultaneously. Graphics processing units (GPUs) excel in data parallelism, making them ideal for tasks like image processing and machine learning.

The field of deep learning has witnessed remarkable advancements, thanks to data parallelism and the utilization of GPUs. Researchers and practitioners can train complex neural networks by dividing the training data across multiple GPUs, enabling faster convergence and more efficient model training. This has led to groundbreaking applications in areas such as image recognition, natural language processing, and autonomous vehicles.

By employing task parallelism and data parallelism, we can unlock the potential of parallel algorithms and achieve significant performance improvements. However, designing effective parallel algorithms requires careful consideration of factors such as load balancing, synchronization, and communication overhead. In the upcoming chapters, we will dive deeper into these aspects and explore real-world examples where parallel algorithms have revolutionized problem-solving across various domains.

Distributed Algorithm Design

Distributed systems introduce unique challenges due to the decentralized nature of computation. Designing algorithms that can effectively operate in such environments requires a deep understanding of communication, synchronization, and fault tolerance. Let's delve into some key aspects of designing distributed algorithms:

Communication and Message Passing: In distributed systems, communication between nodes plays a vital role. Algorithms must utilize efficient message passing protocols to exchange information and coordinate actions. One classic example is the Lamport timestamps algorithm, which enables logical ordering of events in distributed systems. By assigning logical timestamps to messages, this algorithm facilitates causality tracking and synchronization across distributed nodes.

The BitTorrent protocol revolutionized the way we share and distribute large files over the internet. By utilizing distributed algorithms, BitTorrent allows users to download files in small pieces from multiple sources simultaneously. The protocol employs efficient message passing techniques to coordinate the distribution process, making it resilient to network disruptions and ensuring faster downloads.

Synchronization and Consensus: Achieving consensus among distributed nodes is crucial for ensuring the correctness of distributed algorithms. Various consensus algorithms, such as the Paxos algorithm, have been developed to handle scenarios where nodes need to agree on a common value or make collective decisions. These algorithms provide fault-tolerant and robust solutions for distributed coordination.

Blockchain technology, popularized by Bitcoin, relies on distributed consensus algorithms to achieve agreement among participants in a decentralized network. Through mechanisms like Proof-of-Work and Byzantine Fault Tolerance, blockchain networks enable trustless and secure transactions, paving the way for applications beyond cryptocurrencies, such as supply chain management and decentralized finance.

Designing distributed algorithms also involves considerations of fault tolerance, load balancing, and scalability. Balancing the distribution of computational load and ensuring fault-tolerant behavior are critical in distributed systems to maintain system reliability and performance.

By leveraging communication, synchronization, and consensus techniques, distributed algorithms have the potential to transform industries and solve challenges that are beyond the scope of a single machine. In the upcoming chapters, we will delve deeper into real-world examples, explore cutting-edge research, and uncover the remarkable impact of distributed algorithms in various domains.

In parallel and distributed computing, traditional data structures need to be adapted or new data structures need to be designed to ensure efficient data management in a distributed environment. Let's delve into some key aspects of parallel and distributed data structures:

Concurrent Access and Updates: One of the major challenges in parallel and distributed systems is managing concurrent access and updates to shared data. Concurrent data structures, such as concurrent hash tables and lock-free data structures, provide mechanisms to enable multiple threads or processes to access and modify shared data without conflicts. These data structures ensure data integrity while maximizing parallelism and performance.

The Apache Cassandra distributed database is designed to handle massive amounts of data across multiple nodes while ensuring high availability and scalability. Cassandra utilizes a distributed hash table data structure that allows concurrent read and write operations across the distributed cluster. This enables seamless scaling and fault tolerance, making Cassandra a popular choice for global-scale applications.

Load Balancing and Data Partitioning: In distributed systems, load balancing is essential to ensure optimal resource utilization and prevent bottlenecks. Data partitioning techniques, such as consistent hashing, enable the distribution of data across multiple nodes, ensuring balanced workloads and efficient data retrieval. By

```
# Spawn parallel threads
# Each thread calculates the sum of its assigned portion of the array
# Here, we use the OpenMP parallel for directive to parallelize the summation task
# and the OpenMP reduction clause to automatically perform the reduction operation
# to obtain the final sum
# In this example, we assume the existence of a GetThreadID() function
# that returns the unique thread identifier
# and a GetThreadChunk() function that returns the portion of the array
# assigned to each thread
```

```
ParallelSum(array):
    sum = 0

    #pragma omp parallel for reduction(+: sum)
    for i = 0 to length(array) - 1:
        thread_id = GetThreadID()
        thread_chunk = GetThreadChunk(thread_id)

        sum += thread_chunk[i]

    return sum
```

ParallelBinarySearch(array, target):
```
    # Split the array among parallel processes
    # Each process searches a portion of the array
    start_index = compute_start_index()
    end_index = compute_end_index()

    # Perform a binary search on the local portion of the array
    while start_index <= end_index:
        mid = (start_index + end_index) / 2

        if array[mid] == target:
            return mid
        else if array[mid] < target:
            start_index = mid + 1
        else:
            end_index = mid - 1

    # Return -1 if the target is not found
    return -1
```

ParallelMergeSort(array):
```
    if length(array) <= 1:
        return array

    # Divide the array into two halves
    mid = length(array) / 2
    left = array[0:mid]
    right = array[mid:]

    # Launch parallel threads on the GPU
    # Each thread recursively sorts its assigned portion of the array
    sorted_left = ParallelMergeSort(left)
    sorted_right = ParallelMergeSort(right)

    # Merge the sorted halves
    sorted_array = Merge(sorted_left, sorted_right)

    return sorted_array
```

Performance Analysis and Scalability

Performance analysis and scalability assessment are essential in understanding the efficiency and effectiveness of parallel and distributed algorithms. Let's delve into key aspects of performance analysis and scalability and explore techniques that can unleash their potential:

Evaluating Algorithmic Performance: Understanding the performance of parallel and distributed algorithms is crucial in identifying bottlenecks, optimizing resource utilization, and improving overall efficiency. Performance metrics such as execution time, throughput, and scalability play a significant role in assessing algorithmic performance. By analyzing these metrics, we can identify areas of improvement and make informed decisions about algorithm design and implementation.

The Netflix recommendation system is a prime example of performance analysis and optimization. To deliver personalized recommendations to millions of users, Netflix employs complex parallel and distributed algorithms. Through extensive performance analysis, Netflix continuously optimizes their recommendation algorithms, resulting in improved user experience and increased customer satisfaction.

Scalability and its Factors: Scalability refers to the ability of a system to handle increasing workloads and accommodate growth without sacrificing performance. Understanding scalability factors is crucial for designing algorithms that can adapt to growing data sizes, increasing user demands, and evolving system architectures. Factors such as load balancing, communication overhead, and data distribution strategies significantly impact the scalability of parallel and distributed systems.

Measuring and Benchmarking Techniques: Accurately measuring and benchmarking parallel and distributed systems is crucial for performance evaluation and comparison. Techniques such as profiling, tracing, and benchmarking suites help identify performance bottlenecks, evaluate system behavior, and make informed decisions for optimization. These techniques enable developers to fine-tune algorithms and system configurations for maximum efficiency.

The SPEC (Standard Performance Evaluation Corporation) benchmarks are widely used to assess the performance of various computing systems. SPEC benchmarks provide standardized workloads and measurement methodologies, allowing fair comparisons between different hardware and software platforms. These benchmarks have played a pivotal role in evaluating the scalability and performance of parallel and distributed systems.

Scientific Discoveries: Parallel and distributed algorithms have played a pivotal role in advancing scientific research and enabling groundbreaking discoveries. High-performance computing clusters and distributed computing frameworks have empowered scientists to tackle complex simulations, analyze massive datasets, and solve intricate mathematical models. These advancements have led to breakthroughs in areas such as astrophysics, genomics, climate modeling, and drug discovery.

The Folding@home project stands as a prime example of distributed computing driving scientific breakthroughs. By harnessing the collective processing power of volunteers' computers worldwide, Folding@home has contributed to significant advancements in understanding protein folding, leading to breakthroughs in disease research, including Alzheimer's, Parkinson's, and cancer.

Parallel and distributed algorithms have revolutionized the field of big data analytics, enabling organizations to extract valuable insights from vast and complex datasets. MapReduce, Spark, and Hadoop are just a few examples of distributed computing frameworks that have empowered businesses to process and analyze enormous volumes of data in parallel. This has led to significant advancements in areas such as customer analytics, fraud detection, recommendation systems, and sentiment analysis.

7

Graph Algorithms

Graph theory is a fascinating branch of mathematics that deals with the study of graphs, which are mathematical structures consisting of vertices (also known as nodes) connected by edges. Graph theory has a wide range of applications in various fields, including computer science, social networks, transportation systems, and communication networks. In this section, we will delve into the foundational concepts of graph theory and explore its practical applications.

A graph consists of a set of vertices and a set of edges that connect pairs of vertices. Vertices represent entities or objects, while edges represent the relationships or connections between these entities. Graphs can be classified into different types based on their characteristics. For instance, a graph can be directed or undirected, depending on whether the edges have a specific direction or not. It can also be weighted or unweighted, where edges have assigned values or are unweighted. Additionally, graphs can be cyclic or acyclic, with cycles representing loops within the graph structure.

Real-life examples of graph theory's applications are abundant. Consider a social network like Facebook, where individuals are represented as vertices, and their friendships are represented as edges. Graph algorithms can be used to analyze the structure of the social network, identify influential individuals, and recommend friends based on common connections. Similarly, in transportation systems, graphs can model road networks, with vertices representing intersections and edges representing roads. Graph algorithms can help optimize traffic flow, find the shortest routes, and plan efficient delivery routes.

Example

To illustrate the concept of a graph, let's consider a simple undirected graph with four vertices (A, B, C, D) and five edges (AB, AC, BC, CD, BD). We can represent this graph using an adjacency list.

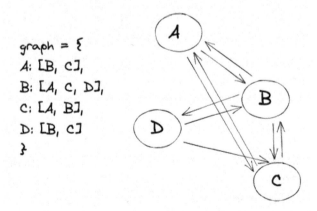

```
graph = {
A: [B, C],
B: [A, C, D],
C: [A, B],
D: [B, C]
}
```

In the above example, each vertex is associated with a list of vertices to which it is directly connected. This representation allows us to efficiently navigate through the graph and perform various graph algorithms.

By understanding the fundamental concepts of graph theory, you will gain a powerful toolkit to solve a wide range of problems. In the upcoming sections, we will explore graph traversal algorithms, shortest path algorithms, and spanning tree algorithms, which leverage the properties of graphs to solve complex problems efficiently.

Graph Traversal Algorithms

Graph traversal algorithms are essential tools for exploring and analyzing the structure of a graph. They allow us to visit all the vertices of a graph in a systematic manner, ensuring that we don't miss any connections or paths. In this section, we will dive into two popular graph traversal algorithms: breadth-first search (BFS) and depth-first search (DFS).

Breadth-First Search (BFS)

BFS is an algorithm that explores a graph by visiting vertices in layers or levels. Starting from a chosen vertex, BFS explores all its adjacent vertices before moving on to the next level. This process continues until all vertices have been visited. BFS is commonly used to find the shortest path between two vertices or to discover the connectivity of a graph.

```
function BFS(graph, start_vertex):
    create a queue
    enqueue start_vertex
    create a set to track visited vertices
    add start_vertex to the set

    while the queue is not empty:
        current_vertex = dequeue from the queue
        process current_vertex

        for each neighbor_vertex adjacent to current_vertex:
            if neighbor_vertex is not in the set of visited vertices:
                enqueue neighbor_vertex
                add neighbor_vertex to the set of visited vertices
```

Depth-First Search (DFS)
DFS explores a graph by traversing as deeply as possible along each branch before backtracking. It visits a vertex, explores all its adjacent vertices, and recursively applies the same process to each unvisited vertex until all vertices have been visited. DFS is commonly used to detect cycles, find connected components, and solve puzzles like mazes.

```
function DFS(graph, start_vertex, visited_set):
    add start_vertex to the visited_set
    process start_vertex

    for each neighbor_vertex adjacent to start_vertex:
        if neighbor_vertex is not in the visited_set:
            DFS(graph, neighbor_vertex, visited_set)
```

Consider a scenario where you are designing a web crawler that needs to visit and index web pages. The web can be represented as a large graph, with each webpage as a vertex and hyperlinks between pages as edges. You can use a graph traversal algorithm like BFS or DFS to systematically explore and index web pages, ensuring that all pages are visited and indexed efficiently.

Understanding graph traversal algorithms is crucial for solving various graph-related problems and exploring complex networks efficiently. In the upcoming sections, we will dive into shortest path algorithms and spanning tree algorithms, which build upon the concepts of graph traversal.

Shortest Path Algorithms

Shortest path algorithms are fundamental in graph theory and have numerous real-world applications. They help us find the most efficient route between two vertices in a graph, considering the weights or costs associated with the edges. In this section, we will explore two popular shortest path algorithms: Dijkstra's algorithm and the Bellman-Ford algorithm.

Dijkstra's Algorithm

Dijkstra's algorithm is a widely used algorithm for finding the shortest path between a source vertex and all other vertices in a weighted graph. It works by maintaining a priority queue of vertices and repeatedly selecting the vertex with the minimum distance from the source. By iteratively updating the distances, Dijkstra's algorithm ensures that the shortest path to each vertex is progressively determined.

```
function Dijkstra(graph, start_vertex):
  #create a priority queue
  #enqueue start_vertex with a distance of 0
  #create a dictionary to track shortest distances
  #initialize all distances to infinity except start_vertex (0)

  while the priority queue is not empty:
    current_vertex = dequeue from the priority queue

    for each neighbor_vertex adjacent to current_vertex:
      calculate new_distance = current_distance + edge_weight(current_vertex, neighbor_vertex)

      if new_distance is smaller than the current distance to neighbor_vertex:
        update the distance to neighbor_vertex to new_distance
        enqueue neighbor_vertex with new_distance into the priority queue
```

Bellman-Ford Algorithm

The Bellman-Ford algorithm is another widely used shortest path algorithm that can handle graphs with negative edge weights. It iterates over all edges multiple times, gradually improving the shortest distance estimates until reaching the optimal solution. The algorithm detects negative cycles and reports if they exist in the graph.

```
function BellmanFord(graph, start_vertex):
 #create a list of distances
 #initialize all distances to infinity except start_vertex (0)

 repeat |V| - 1 times:
   for each edge (u, v) with weight w in the graph:
    if distance[u] + w < distance[v]:
     update the distance[v] to distance[u] + w

   for each edge (u, v) with weight w in the graph:
    if distance[u] + w < distance[v]:
     report a negative cycle exists
```

Imagine you are developing a GPS navigation system that needs to find the shortest path between two locations. By representing the road network as a graph, with intersections as vertices and roads as edges, you can use shortest path algorithms like Dijkstra's algorithm or the Bellman-Ford algorithm to calculate the most efficient route, considering factors such as distance, traffic, or travel time.

Shortest path algorithms have extensive applications in transportation, logistics, network routing, and many other domains. They are crucial tools for optimizing travel routes, finding the most efficient paths, and solving complex optimization problems.

Spanning Tree Algorithms

Spanning tree algorithms play a crucial role in graph theory, allowing us to identify a subset of edges that form a tree connecting all the vertices of a graph. In this section, we will explore two popular spanning tree algorithms: Kruskal's algorithm and Prim's algorithm.

Kruskal's Algorithm

Kruskal's algorithm is a greedy algorithm that aims to find the minimum spanning tree (MST) of a weighted graph. It starts by sorting all the edges in non-decreasing order of their weights. Then, it iterates over the sorted edges and adds them to the MST if they do not create a cycle. Kruskal's algorithm ensures that the MST remains connected and contains the minimum total weight among all possible spanning trees.

```
function Kruskal(graph):
    #create an empty set to store the MST
    #create a disjoint set data structure

    #sort all edges in non-decreasing order of their weights

    for each edge (u, v) in the sorted edges:
        if u and v are not in the same set:
            add the edge (u, v) to the MST
            union the sets containing u and v

    return the MST
```

Prim's Algorithm

Prim's algorithm is another greedy algorithm that finds the minimum spanning tree of a weighted graph. It starts by selecting an arbitrary vertex as the initial node and then repeatedly adds the nearest vertex to the growing MST. The algorithm maintains a priority queue of vertices based on their distances to the current MST. Prim's algorithm guarantees the creation of a connected MST with the minimum total weight.

function Prim(graph):
 #create a priority queue to store vertices
 #create a dictionary to track distances
 #create a dictionary to track parents
 #create a set to store visited vertices

 #select an arbitrary starting vertex
 #set its distance to 0
 #enqueue the starting vertex with a distance of 0

 while the priority queue is not empty:
   current_vertex = dequeue from the priority queue

   if current_vertex is not visited:
     mark current_vertex as visited

     for each neighbor_vertex adjacent to current_vertex:
       if neighbor_vertex is not visited and the edge weight is smaller than its current distance:
         update the distance to neighbor_vertex
         set neighbor_vertex's parent to current_vertex
         enqueue neighbor_vertex with its updated distance

 return the MST

To illustrate the significance of spanning tree algorithms, consider a power distribution network. The network consists of multiple power stations connected by transmission lines. To ensure efficient power distribution and minimize costs, it is essential to identify a minimum spanning tree that connects all the power stations while minimizing the total length or cost of transmission lines. Spanning tree algorithms, such as Kruskal's algorithm or Prim's algorithm, can help optimize the construction and maintenance of power distribution networks.

Spanning tree algorithms also find applications in network design, circuit layout planning, and cluster analysis, among others. They provide a foundation for solving optimization problems where connectivity and resource allocation are essential factors.

Graph Coloring Algorithms

Graph coloring is a fundamental problem in graph theory where the objective is to assign colors to the vertices of a graph such that no two adjacent vertices have the same color. This concept has practical applications in various fields, including scheduling, register allocation in compilers, and frequency assignment in wireless communication. In this section, we will explore some graph coloring algorithms, including the greedy algorithm and the backtracking algorithm.

Greedy Algorithm

The greedy algorithm is a simple and intuitive approach to graph coloring. It works by iteratively selecting a vertex and assigning it the smallest possible color that is not already assigned to its adjacent vertices. This algorithm does not guarantee an optimal solution but often provides a reasonable coloring in practice.

```
function GreedyColoring(graph):
    #create an array to store the color assignments for each vertex
    #initialize all colors to 0 (unassigned)

    for each vertex v in the graph:
        create a set to store the colors of adjacent vertices
        for each neighbor u of v:
            if the color of u is assigned:
                add the color of u to the set

        for each color c in a sequential order:
            if c is not present in the set of adjacent colors:
                assign color c to vertex v
                break
```

Graph coloring algorithms find practical applications in various scheduling problems. For example, consider a university timetable scheduling where courses are represented as vertices and conflicts between courses are represented as edges. By assigning different colors to courses that have overlapping schedules, the timetable can be constructed to ensure that no two conflicting courses are scheduled at the same time.

In wireless communication, graph coloring is used to assign different frequencies to nearby cell towers or Wi-Fi access points to avoid interference. By assigning different colors (frequencies) to neighboring transmitters, the communication channels can operate simultaneously without causing interference.

8

Computational Thinking

Understanding Computational Thinking

Computational thinking is a fundamental approach to problem-solving that draws inspiration from computer science principles. It involves breaking down complex problems into smaller, more manageable parts and employing logical reasoning to devise efficient solutions. In this section, we will explore the definition and significance of computational thinking, the core components that constitute it, and the benefits of applying computational thinking in problem-solving.

Computational thinking refers to the cognitive processes and strategies employed to solve problems, design systems, and understand human behavior through the lens of computer science. It encompasses a set of skills and techniques that enable individuals to approach problems in a systematic and structured manner.

By employing computational thinking, individuals learn to analyze problems, identify patterns and similarities, devise algorithms, and leverage data representation and abstraction to develop efficient solutions. It is a mindset that goes beyond programming and is applicable in various domains, from scientific research to business optimization.

Core Components of Computational Thinking
Computational thinking involves several key components that form the foundation of problem-solving:

Decomposition: Breaking down complex problems into smaller, more manageable tasks. This process enables individuals to focus on individual components and develop solutions incrementally.

Pattern Recognition: Identifying similarities, trends, and patterns in problem instances. Recognizing patterns allows for the application of existing solutions or the development of new approaches based on observed patterns.

Abstraction: Removing unnecessary details and focusing on the essential elements of a problem. Abstraction allows individuals to create generalized models and algorithms that can be applied to various problem instances.

Algorithmic Design: Developing step-by-step plans or algorithms to solve problems. Algorithmic design involves creating clear and unambiguous instructions that can be executed to achieve the desired outcome.

Logical Reasoning: Evaluating information, making inferences, and drawing conclusions based on logical principles. Logical reasoning ensures that solutions are rational, consistent, and free from contradictions.

Data Representation: Organizing and manipulating information in a structured manner. Effective data representation allows for efficient storage, retrieval, and manipulation of data during problem-solving.

These components work together synergistically to enable individuals to approach problems with a computational mindset.

Computational thinking offers numerous benefits that extend beyond computer science:

Problem-solving skills: Computational thinking equips individuals with a systematic approach to problem-solving, enabling them to tackle complex issues more effectively.

Analytical thinking: By breaking down problems and identifying patterns, computational thinking enhances analytical skills, fostering a deeper understanding of problem domains.

Efficiency and scalability: Computational thinking encourages the development of efficient algorithms and solutions, leading to improved efficiency and scalability in problem-solving.

Transferable skills: Computational thinking skills are applicable in various domains, allowing individuals to apply their problem-solving abilities to diverse contexts.

Creativity and innovation: Computational thinking fosters creativity by encouraging individuals to think outside the box, explore alternative solutions, and develop innovative approaches to problems.

NASA's Mars Rover Missions
The Mars Rover missions by NASA exemplify the power of computational thinking in solving complex problems. When designing the autonomous rovers to explore the Martian surface, NASA engineers had to overcome numerous challenges, such as navigating rough terrain, collecting samples, and analyzing data. By employing computational thinking principles, they decomposed the mission into smaller tasks, designed algorithms for obstacle avoidance and sample collection, utilized pattern recognition to identify features of interest, and employed logical reasoning to interpret data. These missions stand as a testament to the effectiveness of computational thinking in achieving remarkable scientific advancements.

The pseudo code demonstrates the logical and systematic approach to finding the maximum number in a list using iterative comparison. This algorithm showcases the core components of computational thinking, including decomposition (iterating through the list), logical reasoning (comparing elements), and algorithmic design (updating the maximum value).

By understanding the definition, core components, and benefits of computational thinking, you will be equipped with a powerful problem-solving approach. Embracing computational thinking empowers you to break down complex problems, recognize patterns, design efficient algorithms, and leverage logical reasoning to arrive at effective solutions.

Let's continue our journey of developing an algorithmic mindset in the chapters ahead.

9

Algorithm Design Patterns

Design patterns are reusable solutions to common problems that occur in software design and development. They provide a structured approach to solving recurring design challenges, offering proven solutions that have been refined and validated over time by experienced software designers and developers. Design patterns serve as blueprints that capture the essence of solving specific design problems, providing guidance on how to approach and implement solutions.

To understand design patterns better, let's consider an analogy. Think of a design pattern as a recipe for baking a cake. Just as a recipe provides step-by-step instructions on how to create a delicious cake, a design pattern provides a set of guidelines and best practices for solving a particular design problem in software development. It offers a standardized approach that has been proven to work effectively in various scenarios.

Importance of Design Patterns in Software Development
Design patterns play a crucial role in software development for several reasons. Firstly, they promote code reusability. By encapsulating common design solutions, design patterns enable developers to reuse proven approaches rather than reinventing them each time. This saves development time and effort, and also reduces the risk of introducing errors or suboptimal designs.

Secondly, design patterns enhance code maintainability. They provide a shared vocabulary and standardized structure, making it easier for developers to understand and work with code that follows recognized patterns. This improves collaboration and reduces the learning curve when developers need to modify or enhance existing codebases.

Moreover, design patterns contribute to code extensibility and flexibility. They provide a framework for building software systems that can accommodate future changes and new requirements. By applying design patterns, developers can design modular and loosely coupled components, making it easier to adapt and evolve the software over time.

Benefits of Using Design Patterns
Using design patterns in software development offers numerous benefits that positively impact the overall quality and efficiency of the development process.

One significant benefit is improved code quality. Design patterns encourage the use of established best practices and design principles, leading to cleaner, more organized code. This makes the code easier to read, understand, and maintain, reducing the likelihood of bugs and facilitating future enhancements.

Additionally, design patterns facilitate code scalability and performance optimization. They provide efficient and proven algorithms and data structures that can handle large-scale data processing and complex operations. For example, the Singleton design pattern ensures that only one instance of a class exists, which can be useful in scenarios where limited resources need to be managed efficiently.

Furthermore, design patterns promote code modularity and separation of concerns. By structuring code around well-defined patterns, developers can isolate different aspects of the system and make them easier to manage, test, and debug. This improves code comprehensibility and facilitates code reuse.

Real-life examples of design patterns can be found in popular software frameworks and libraries. For instance, the Model-View-Controller (MVC) design pattern is widely used in web development frameworks like Ruby on Rails and Laravel. It separates the application's data model, user interface, and business logic, enabling a clean and maintainable architecture.

In conclusion, design patterns are invaluable tools in software development. They provide reusable and proven solutions to common design challenges, promoting code reusability, maintainability, and scalability. By incorporating design patterns into their development practices, programmers can elevate their software design skills and create robust and efficient software systems.

Creational Design Patterns

In this section, we will explore several creational design patterns that focus on creating objects in a flexible and efficient manner. These patterns provide solutions for object instantiation and initialization, allowing developers to create objects in a way that suits the specific requirements of their applications. We will discuss the Singleton pattern, Factory pattern, Abstract Factory pattern, Builder pattern, and Prototype pattern.

Singleton Pattern

The Singleton pattern ensures that a class has only one instance and provides a global point of access to it. This pattern is useful when you want to limit the number of instances of a class and ensure that all clients access the same instance. It is commonly used for managing shared resources, such as database connections or loggers.

Pseudo-code example of the Singleton pattern:

```
class Singleton:
    _instance = None

    def __new__(cls):
        if cls._instance is None:
            cls._instance = super().__new__(cls)
        return cls._instance
```

A real-life example of the Singleton pattern is the Logger class in a logging framework. There should be only one instance of the Logger class throughout the application to ensure consistent logging behavior.

Factory Pattern

The Factory pattern provides an interface for creating objects without specifying their concrete classes. It encapsulates the object creation logic in a separate class, which is responsible for instantiating the appropriate objects based on certain conditions or parameters. This pattern promotes loose coupling between the client and the object creation process, allowing for easier extensibility and maintenance.

Pseudo-code example of the Factory pattern:

```python
class Product:
  def operation(self):
    pass

class ConcreteProduct1(Product):
  def operation(self):
    # Perform operation specific to ConcreteProduct1
    pass

class ConcreteProduct2(Product):
  def operation(self):
    # Perform operation specific to ConcreteProduct2
    pass

class Factory:
  def create_product(self):
    pass

class ConcreteFactory1(Factory):
  def create_product(self):
    return ConcreteProduct1()

class ConcreteFactory2(Factory):
  def create_product(self):
    return ConcreteProduct2()
```

A real-life example of the Factory pattern is a GUI framework that provides different types of buttons (e.g., WindowsButton, MacButton) based on the user's operating system.

Abstract Factory Pattern

The Abstract Factory pattern provides an interface for creating families of related or dependent objects. It allows clients to create objects without specifying their concrete classes, similar to the Factory pattern. However, the Abstract Factory pattern emphasizes the creation of families of objects, ensuring that the resulting objects are compatible with each other.

Pseudo-code example of the Abstract Factory pattern:

```python
class AbstractProductA:
  def operation(self):
    pass

class AbstractProductB:
  def operation(self):
    pass

class ConcreteProductA1(AbstractProductA):
  def operation(self):
    # Perform operation specific to ConcreteProductA1
    pass

class ConcreteProductA2(AbstractProductA):
  def operation(self):
    # Perform operation specific to ConcreteProductA2
    pass

class ConcreteProductB1(AbstractProductB):
  def operation(self):
    # Perform operation specific to ConcreteProductB1
    pass

class ConcreteProductB2(AbstractProductB):
  def operation(self):
    # Perform operation specific to ConcreteProductB2
    pass

class AbstractFactory:
  def create_product_a(self):
    pass

  def create_product_b(self):
    pass

class ConcreteFactory1(AbstractFactory):
  def create_product_a(self):
    return ConcreteProductA1()

  def create_product_b(self):
    return ConcreteProductB1()

class ConcreteFactory2(AbstractFactory):
  def create_product_a(self):
    return ConcreteProduct

A2()

  def create_product_b(self):
    return ConcreteProductB2()
```

A real-life example of the Abstract Factory pattern is a UI framework that provides different components (e.g., buttons, text boxes, menus) for different operating systems (e.g., Windows, Mac, Linux) while ensuring compatibility between the components.

Builder Pattern

The Builder pattern separates the construction of complex objects from their representation, allowing the same construction process to create different representations. It provides a step-by-step approach to construct objects by abstracting the construction process and allowing for the creation of complex objects with varying configurations.

Pseudo-code example of the Builder pattern:

```python
class Product:
    def __init__(self):
        self.part1 = None
        self.part2 = None

class Builder:
    def build_part1(self):
        pass

    def build_part2(self):
        pass

    def get_product(self):
        pass

class ConcreteBuilder(Builder):
    def __init__(self):
        self.product = Product()

    def build_part1(self):
        self.product.part1 = "Part 1"

    def build_part2(self):
        self.product.part2 = "Part 2"

    def get_product(self):
        return self.product

class Director:
    def construct(self, builder):
        builder.build_part1()
        builder.build_part2()
        return builder.get_product()
```

A real-life example of the Builder pattern is a document editor that allows users to construct complex documents with various sections, paragraphs, and formatting options.

Prototype Pattern
The Prototype pattern involves creating new objects by cloning existing objects, avoiding the need for explicit object creation using a constructor. It allows for the creation of new objects with different initial states by cloning a prototype object. This pattern is beneficial when creating objects is costly or complex, and the initial state of the objects varies.

Pseudo-code example of the Prototype pattern:

```python
import copy

class Prototype:
    def clone(self):
        pass

class ConcretePrototype(Prototype):
    def __init__(self, data):
        self.data = data

    def clone(self):
        return copy.deepcopy(self)

# Usage
prototype = ConcretePrototype("Initial data")
clone = prototype.clone()
```

A real-life example of the Prototype pattern is a word processor that allows users to create multiple copies of a document by cloning an existing document, enabling them to start with a predefined structure and make modifications as needed.

By understanding and utilizing these creational design patterns, you will be equipped with powerful tools to create objects efficiently and flexibly in your software development projects. These patterns promote code reuse, maintainability, and scalability, making your applications more robust and adaptable to changing requirements.

Structural Design Patterns

In this section, we will delve into various structural design patterns that focus on the composition and organization of classes and objects. These patterns provide solutions for creating relationships between objects and structuring them in a way that enhances flexibility, maintainability, and extensibility. We will explore the Adapter pattern, Bridge pattern, Composite pattern, Decorator pattern, Facade pattern, and Proxy pattern.

Adapter Pattern

The Adapter pattern allows objects with incompatible interfaces to work together by providing a common interface that both objects can use. It acts as a bridge between the existing code and the desired interface, enabling communication and collaboration between different components.

Pseudo-code example of the Adapter pattern:

```
class Target:
   def request(self):
      pass

class Adaptee:
   def specific_request(self):
      pass

class Adapter(Target):
   def __init__(self, adaptee):
      self.adaptee = adaptee

   def request(self):
      self.adaptee.specific_request()
```

A real-life example of the Adapter pattern is a power adapter that allows electronic devices with different plug types to be used in different countries' electrical outlets.

Bridge Pattern
The Bridge pattern decouples an abstraction from its implementation, allowing both to vary independently. It separates the abstraction's interface from its implementation details, enabling changes in one without affecting the other. This pattern promotes flexibility and extensibility by providing a clear separation between different aspects of a system.

Pseudo-code example of the Bridge pattern:

```
class Abstraction:
    def __init__(self, implementation):
        self.implementation = implementation

    def operation(self):
        self.implementation.operation_implementation()

class Implementation:
    def operation_implementation(self):
        pass

class ConcreteImplementationA(Implementation):
    def operation_implementation(self):
        # Perform operation specific to ConcreteImplementationA
        pass

class ConcreteImplementationB(Implementation):
    def operation_implementation(self):
        # Perform operation specific to ConcreteImplementationB
        pass
```

A real-life example of the Bridge pattern is a remote control for a television. The remote control acts as an abstraction, while the different television models serve as implementations that can be changed or upgraded independently.

Composite Pattern

The Composite pattern composes objects into tree structures to represent part-whole hierarchies. It allows clients to treat individual objects and compositions of objects uniformly. This pattern simplifies the client's code by providing a consistent interface to work with both individual objects and groups of objects.

Pseudo-code example of the Composite pattern:

```
class Component:
  def operation(self):
    pass

class Leaf(Component):
  def operation(self):
    # Perform operation specific to Leaf
    pass

class Composite(Component):
  def __init__(self):
    self.children = []

  def add_child(self, child):
    self.children.append(child)

  def remove_child(self, child):
    self.children.remove(child)

  def operation(self):
    for child in self.children:
      child.operation()
```

A real-life example of the Composite pattern is a file system where directories can contain files and other directories. The file system can be traversed and manipulated uniformly, regardless of whether the element is a file or a directory.

Decorator Pattern

The Decorator pattern allows behavior to be added to an object dynamically, extending its functionality without modifying its structure. It provides a flexible alternative to subclassing, enabling objects to gain new features by wrapping them with decorator objects.

Pseudo-code example of the Decorator pattern:

```python
class Component:
    def operation(self):
        pass

class ConcreteComponent(Component):
    def operation(self):
        # Perform operation specific to ConcreteComponent
        pass

class Decorator(Component):
    def __init__(self, component):
        self.component = component

    def operation(self):
        self.component.operation()

class ConcreteDecorator(Decorator):
    def operation(self):
        # Perform additional operation before or after calling the wrapped
object's operation
        super().operation()
        # Perform additional operation after calling the wrapped object's
operation
```

A real-life example of the Decorator pattern is a text processing application that allows users to add formatting options (e.g., bold, italic) to text dynamically without modifying the original text.

Facade Pattern

The Facade pattern provides a simplified interface to a complex subsystem, encapsulating its complexity behind a single interface. It acts as a high-level interface that hides the complexities of the underlying system, making it easier for clients to use and reducing dependencies between the client code and the subsystem.

Pseudo-code example of the Facade pattern:

```python
class SubsystemA:
    def operation_a(self):
        pass

class SubsystemB:
    def operation_b(self):
        pass

class Facade:
    def __init__(self):
        self.subsystem_a = SubsystemA()
        self.subsystem_b = SubsystemB()

    def operation(self):
        self.subsystem_a.operation_a()
        self.subsystem_b.operation_b()
```

A real-life example of the Facade pattern is a multimedia player that provides a single interface to play different types of media files (e.g., audio, video) without the client needing to understand the intricacies of each media format.

Proxy Pattern

The Proxy pattern provides a surrogate or placeholder for another object to control access to it. It allows for the creation of an intermediary object that acts as a substitute for the real object, providing additional functionality, such as lazy initialization, access control, or remote communication.

Pseudo-code example of the Proxy pattern:

```
class Subject:
    def request(self):
        pass

class RealSubject(Subject):
    def request(self):
        # Perform the real request
        pass

class Proxy(Subject):
    def __init__(self, real_subject):
        self.real_subject = real_subject

    def request(self):
        # Perform pre-processing before forwarding the request to the real subject
        self.real_subject.request()
        # Perform post-processing after the request has been handled by the real subject
```

A real-life example of the Proxy pattern is a remote proxy that acts as a local representative for an object located in a remote system. The proxy handles the communication between the client and the remote object, providing a seamless experience for the client.

By understanding and applying these structural design patterns, you will gain valuable techniques to organize and structure your software components effectively, ensuring flexibility, maintainability, and extensibility in your applications.

Behavioral Design Patterns

In this section, we will explore various behavioral design patterns that focus on defining the interaction between objects and the behavior of individual objects within a system. These patterns provide solutions for creating flexible and maintainable software by promoting loose coupling and encapsulating behavior in separate objects. We will discuss the Observer pattern, Strategy pattern, Template Method pattern, Iterator pattern, State pattern, Command pattern, and Visitor pattern.

Observer Pattern

The Observer pattern establishes a one-to-many dependency between objects, where multiple observers are notified and updated automatically when the state of a subject object changes. This pattern decouples the subject from its observers, allowing for loosely coupled and easily maintainable systems.

Pseudo-code example of the Observer pattern:

```python
class Subject:
    def __init__(self):
        self.observers = []

    def attach(self, observer):
        self.observers.append(observer)

    def detach(self, observer):
        self.observers.remove(observer)

    def notify(self):
        for observer in self.observers:
            observer.update()

class Observer:
    def update(self):
        pass

class ConcreteSubject(Subject):
    def __init__(self):
        super().__init__()
        self.state = None

    def set_state(self, state):
        self.state = state
        self.notify()

class ConcreteObserver(Observer):
    def update(self):
        # Perform necessary actions based on the updated state of the subject
        pass
```

A real-life example of the Observer pattern is a news agency that broadcasts news updates to multiple subscribers. When news is published, all subscribers are notified automatically.

Strategy Pattern

The Strategy pattern defines a family of interchangeable algorithms and encapsulates each algorithm, allowing them to be used interchangeably within a context. It enables dynamic selection of algorithms at runtime and promotes flexibility and maintainability by separating algorithms from the client code.

Pseudo-code example of the Strategy pattern:

```
class Context:
    def __init__(self, strategy):
        self.strategy = strategy

    def do_operation(self):
        self.strategy.algorithm()

class Strategy:
    def algorithm(self):
        pass

class ConcreteStrategyA(Strategy):
    def algorithm(self):
        # Implement algorithm A
        pass

class ConcreteStrategyB(Strategy):
    def algorithm(self):
        # Implement algorithm B
        pass
```

A real-life example of the Strategy pattern is a sorting algorithm. Different sorting algorithms (e.g., bubble sort, merge sort) can be encapsulated as strategies, and the appropriate strategy can be selected based on the size or type of data being sorted.

Template Method Pattern
The Template Method pattern defines the skeleton of an algorithm in a superclass but allows subclasses to override specific steps of the algorithm. It provides a way to define a common algorithm structure while allowing subclasses to provide custom implementations for certain steps.

Pseudo-code example of the Template Method pattern:

```python
class AbstractClass:
    def template_method(self):
        self.step_1()
        self.step_2()
        self.step_3()

    def step_1(self):
        pass

    def step_2(self):
        pass

    def step_3(self):
        pass

class ConcreteClass(AbstractClass):
    def step_1(self):
        # Implement step 1 specific to ConcreteClass

    def step_2(self):
        # Implement step 2 specific to ConcreteClass

    def step_3(self):
        # Implement step 3 specific to ConcreteClass
```

A real-life example of the Template Method pattern is a recipe. The recipe provides a template for preparing a dish, with specific steps that can be customized based on the dish being prepared.

Iterator Pattern
The Iterator pattern provides a way to access elements

of an aggregate object sequentially without exposing its underlying representation. It separates the traversal logic from the aggregate object, promoting encapsulation and flexibility.

Pseudo-code example of the Iterator pattern:

```
class Iterator:
  def has_next(self):
    pass

  def next(self):
    pass

class ConcreteIterator(Iterator):
  def __init__(self, collection):
    self.collection = collection
    self.index = 0

  def has_next(self):
    return self.index < len(self.collection)

  def next(self):
    if self.has_next():
      item = self.collection[self.index]
      self.index += 1
      return item

class Aggregate:
  def create_iterator(self):
    pass

class ConcreteAggregate(Aggregate):
  def __init__(self):
    self.collection = []

  def create_iterator(self):
    return ConcreteIterator(self.collection)
```

A real-life example of the Iterator pattern is a music playlist. The playlist can be represented as an aggregate object, and the iterator allows you to iterate over the songs in the playlist sequentially.

State Pattern
The State pattern allows an object to alter its behavior when its internal state changes. It encapsulates different behaviors into separate state objects and enables dynamic switching of states at runtime, promoting extensibility and flexibility.

Pseudo-code example of the State pattern:

```
class Context:
    def __init__(self, state):
        self.state = state

    def request(self):
        self.state.handle()

class State:
    def handle(self):
        pass

class ConcreteStateA(State):
    def handle(self):
        # Implement behavior for State A

class ConcreteStateB(State):
    def handle(self):
        # Implement behavior for State B
```

A real-life example of the State pattern is a vending machine. The vending machine can have different states (e.g., Ready, Dispensing, Out of stock), and its behavior changes based on its current state.

Command Pattern
The Command pattern encapsulates a request as an object, allowing you to parameterize clients with different requests, queue or log requests, and support undo operations. It separates the sender of a request from the object that performs the actual operation, promoting loose coupling and flexibility.

Pseudo-code example of the Command pattern:

```python
class Command:
    def execute(self):
        pass

class Receiver:
    def action(self):
        pass

class ConcreteCommand(Command):
    def __init__(self, receiver):
        self.receiver = receiver

    def execute(self):
        self.receiver.action()

class Invoker:
    def __init__(self):
        self.command = None

    def set_command(self, command):
        self.command = command

    def execute_command(self):
        self.command.execute()
```

A real-life example of the Command pattern is a remote control for electronic devices. The remote control sends commands to different devices (e.g., TV, stereo), and the devices execute the corresponding actions.

Visitor Pattern

The Visitor pattern allows for adding new operations to existing object structures without modifying the structure itself. It separates the operations from the objects on which they operate, promoting extensibility and reducing dependencies.

Pseudo-code example of the Visitor pattern:

```python
class Visitor:
    def visit_element_a(self, element_a):
        pass

    def visit_element_b(self, element_b):
        pass

class Element:
    def accept(self, visitor):
        pass

class ConcreteElementA(Element):
    def accept(self, visitor):
        visitor.visit_element_a(self)

class ConcreteElementB(Element):
    def accept(self, visitor):
        visitor.visit_element_b(self)

class ConcreteVisitor(Visitor):
    def visit_element_a(self, element_a):
        # Implement operation for Element A

    def visit_element_b(self, element_b):
        # Implement operation for Element B
```

A real-life example of the Visitor pattern is a document processor. Different document elements (e.g., paragraphs, images) can accept a visitor that performs specific operations (e.g., formatting, analyzing) on those elements.

By understanding and utilizing these behavioral design patterns, you will be able to design software that is more flexible, maintainable, and extensible. These patterns provide solutions for common design problems and promote best practices in software development.

Architectural Design Patterns

In this section, we will explore several architectural design patterns that provide structure and organization to software systems. These patterns define the overall architecture of an application and address key concerns such as separation of concerns, modularity, and testability. By understanding and applying these patterns, you can design scalable, maintainable, and robust software solutions.

MVC (Model-View-Controller) Pattern

The Model-View-Controller (MVC) pattern is a widely used architectural pattern that separates the application into three interconnected components: the Model, the View, and the Controller. The Model represents the application's data and business logic, the View displays the data to the user, and the Controller handles user input and orchestrates interactions between the Model and the View.

The MVC pattern promotes separation of concerns, making the application easier to understand, maintain, and modify. It enables efficient collaboration between developers working on different components of the application and allows for reusability of code.

Real-life example: One popular example of the MVC pattern is web development frameworks like Ruby on Rails, where the Model represents the database schema and business logic, the View is responsible for rendering HTML templates, and the Controller handles incoming requests and updates the Model accordingly.

MVVM (Model-View-ViewModel) Pattern

The Model-View-ViewModel (MVVM) pattern is an architectural pattern that is particularly useful for designing user interfaces. It extends the concepts of the MVC pattern and introduces a ViewModel component that acts as an intermediary between the Model and the View. The ViewModel provides data and behavior to the View, allowing for a clean separation of concerns and enabling easier testing and maintainability.

The MVVM pattern is commonly used in modern application development frameworks, especially those that utilize data binding capabilities. It promotes a reactive programming style, where changes in the Model automatically update the ViewModel and subsequently reflect in the View.

Real-life example: The MVVM pattern is frequently used in

frameworks like Microsoft's WPF (Windows Presentation Foundation) and Xamarin.Forms for building cross-platform applications. The ViewModel in MVVM corresponds to the application logic and data manipulation, while the View handles the visual representation of the data.

Repository Pattern
The Repository pattern is an architectural pattern that provides an abstraction layer between the application and the data storage. It encapsulates the logic for data retrieval, storage, and querying, and provides a consistent interface for accessing data. By utilizing the Repository pattern, you can decouple the application from specific data access technologies and improve the testability and maintainability of your codebase.

The Repository pattern promotes separation of concerns and enables a clear separation between business logic and data access logic. It also allows for easy switching between different data storage technologies without affecting the application's functionality.

Real-life example: In a web application, the Repository pattern can be used to abstract the underlying database operations. The Repository acts as a bridge between the application and the database, providing methods to query, insert, update, and delete data.

Dependency Injection Pattern
The Dependency Injection (DI) pattern is an architectural pattern that aims to reduce the coupling between

components by removing the responsibility of creating dependencies from the dependent objects. Instead of creating dependencies internally, objects rely on an external entity, known as a dependency injector, to provide the necessary dependencies.

By utilizing the Dependency Injection pattern, you can enhance the modularity and testability of your code. It enables you to easily replace or modify dependencies without impacting the dependent objects, promotes code reusability, and facilitates the implementation of inversion of control (IoC) principles.

Real-life example: Frameworks like Spring (Java) and Angular (JavaScript) employ the Dependency Injection pattern to manage object dependencies. In these frameworks, dependencies are configured and injected into objects using annotations or configuration files.

Service Locator Pattern
The Service Locator pattern is an architectural pattern that provides a centralized registry or container for locating and retrieving services or dependencies required by an application. Instead of direct coupling between components, the Service Locator acts as an intermediary, managing the creation and retrieval of services.

The Service Locator pattern promotes loose coupling between components and allows for better flexibility and maintainability. It centralizes the management of dependencies, making it easier to replace or modify services without modifying the dependent objects.

Real-life example: In a large enterprise application, a Service Locator can be used to locate and retrieve services such as authentication, logging, and database access. This decouples the application components from the specific implementations of these services and enables easier testing and integration.

By understanding and leveraging these architectural design patterns, you can design software systems that are modular, scalable, and maintainable. These patterns provide proven solutions to common architectural challenges and are widely adopted in various software development domains.

Anti-Patterns

In this section, we will explore common pitfalls and anti-patterns in software design that can hinder the maintainability, scalability, and overall quality of software systems. By understanding these anti-patterns and learning how to recognize and avoid them, you can improve the design and longevity of your software projects.

Common Pitfalls in Software Design

Software design is a complex process, and even experienced developers can fall into common pitfalls that can lead to suboptimal solutions. These pitfalls include:

1. God Object: A God Object is a class or component that becomes excessively large and takes on too many responsibilities. This violates the Single Responsibility Principle and makes the codebase difficult to understand, test, and maintain.

2. Spaghetti Code: Spaghetti Code refers to code that is highly tangled and lacks proper structure or organization. It typically arises from poor modularization, excessive dependencies, and lack of separation of concerns.

3. Tight Coupling: Tight Coupling occurs when components are highly dependent on each other, making it difficult to modify or replace one component without affecting others. This can lead to rigid and fragile code that is difficult to extend or maintain.

Recognizing and Avoiding Anti-Patterns

Recognizing and understanding anti-patterns is crucial for avoiding them in your software design. Some strategies to identify and avoid anti-patterns include:

1. Code Reviews: Regular code reviews can help identify potential anti-patterns early in the development process. Peer review can provide valuable feedback and ensure that best practices are followed.

2. Continuous Learning: Keeping up with industry best practices, design principles, and software architecture patterns can help you recognize anti-patterns and make informed design decisions.

3. Refactoring: Refactoring is the process of restructuring existing code without changing its external behavior. It can help address anti-patterns by improving code organization, removing duplication, and reducing coupling.

Refactoring Techniques to Address Anti-Patterns
Refactoring is a key technique for addressing anti-patterns and improving the quality of your code. Some common refactoring techniques include:

1. Extract Class: When a class becomes too large or has multiple responsibilities, you can extract cohesive subsets of functionality into separate classes, following the Single Responsibility Principle.

2. Dependency Injection: By applying the Dependency Injection pattern, you can reduce tight coupling and improve testability and maintainability. Dependencies are injected into objects rather than being created internally.

3. Replace Conditional with Polymorphism: If you find yourself dealing with complex conditional logic, consider using polymorphism to encapsulate behavior within separate classes. This promotes extensibility and simplifies code maintenance.

One common anti-pattern is the "Copy-Paste Programming" where developers repeatedly copy and paste code instead of creating reusable functions or classes. This can lead to code duplication and maintenance challenges. By recognizing this anti-pattern, developers can refactor the code to extract common functionality into reusable functions or classes.

By being aware of these common pitfalls, recognizing anti-patterns, and applying refactoring techniques, you can improve the quality, maintainability, and scalability of your software projects.

Design Patterns in Software Architecture

In this section, we will explore design patterns that are specifically tailored for creating scalable and maintainable software architectures. These patterns provide guidance and best practices for structuring your software systems in a way that promotes modularity, flexibility, and extensibility.

Design Patterns for Scalable and Maintainable Software Architecture

Scalability and maintainability are essential considerations when designing software architecture. By applying the following design patterns, you can create robust and adaptable systems:

1. Layered Architecture Pattern: The Layered Architecture pattern organizes the system into horizontal layers, each responsible for specific functionalities. This pattern promotes separation of concerns and modularity, making it easier to manage and maintain large-scale applications.

The layers typically include presentation, business logic, and data access layers.

2. Microservices Architecture Pattern: The Microservices Architecture pattern decomposes the system into small, independent services that can be developed, deployed, and scaled individually. This pattern promotes flexibility, scalability, and resilience. Each microservice focuses on a specific business capability and communicates with other services through lightweight protocols such as REST or messaging queues.

3. Event-driven Architecture Pattern: The Event-driven Architecture pattern revolves around the concept of events and event processing. It allows different components of the system to communicate asynchronously by producing and consuming events. This pattern enables loose coupling, scalability, and responsiveness, making it suitable for systems that handle high volumes of events and need to react to changes in real-time.

Layered Architecture Pattern
The Layered Architecture pattern divides the system into logical layers, with each layer having a specific responsibility. The layers can be organized as follows:

1. Presentation Layer: The Presentation Layer handles user interaction and interface rendering. It is responsible for capturing user inputs and displaying information to users.

This layer can consist of user interfaces, web services, or APIs.

2. Business Logic Layer: The Business Logic Layer contains the core logic and rules of the application. It processes and manipulates data, enforces business rules, and coordinates the overall flow of the application. This layer encapsulates the business logic, ensuring it is separate from the presentation and data access layers.

3. Data Access Layer: The Data Access Layer is responsible for interacting with the underlying data storage or external services. It handles data retrieval, storage, and manipulation. This layer can include databases, file systems, or external APIs.

By organizing the system into these layers, you can achieve separation of concerns, maintainability, and flexibility. Each layer can be developed and tested independently, allowing for easier maintenance and future modifications.

Microservices Architecture Pattern
The Microservices Architecture pattern decomposes the system into small, autonomous services that can be developed, deployed, and scaled independently. Each microservice focuses on a specific business capability and can communicate with other services through well-defined APIs. Some key aspects of this pattern include:

- Service Independence: Each microservice operates independently, with its own codebase, data storage, and deployment. This enables teams to work on different services concurrently and deploy updates without impacting the entire system.

- Polyglot Architecture: Microservices allow flexibility in technology choices. Each service can be implemented using different programming languages, frameworks, and databases, based on the specific requirements of that service.

- Scalability and Resilience: With the ability to scale individual services, the Microservices Architecture pattern supports horizontal scalability, allowing you to handle increased loads efficiently. Additionally, if one service fails, it doesn't affect the entire system, promoting resilience.

Event-driven Architecture Pattern
The Event-driven Architecture pattern is centered around the concept of events and asynchronous communication. Events represent significant occurrences or changes within the system, and components can produce or consume these events. Key elements of this pattern include:

- Event Producers: Components that generate and publish events when certain conditions or actions occur. These events can be domain-specific events or system events.

- Event Consumers: Components that subscribe to and process events of interest. They react to events and perform actions based on the received information.

- Event Bus: The communication channel through which events are published and consumed. It facilitates the decoupling of event producers and consumers.

A popular example of the Event-driven Architecture pattern is a real-time analytics system. Multiple services or components can generate events when certain actions or events occur, such as user interactions or system updates. These events are then processed by other components, such as analytics engines, which aggregate and analyze the data in real-time.

10

Ethics and Algorithmic Bias

Algorithms have become integral to our daily lives, influencing the decisions that shape our experiences and opportunities. However, these algorithms are not immune to ethical considerations, and their impact on society can be both profound and complex. In this section, we will explore the ethical implications of algorithms and the responsibilities we have as designers, developers, and users.

Algorithms are not neutral—they reflect the biases and values embedded in their design. As a result, they can perpetuate societal biases and reinforce existing inequalities. The field of algorithmic ethics examines the ethical implications of algorithmic decision-making and aims to address issues such as fairness, accountability, transparency, and privacy.

The ProPublica study on the COMPAS algorithm used in the criminal justice system revealed significant racial bias in predicting recidivism rates. African-American defendants were more likely to be falsely identified as high risk compared to their white counterparts. This example highlights the need for algorithmic accountability and ethical scrutiny.

Holding algorithms accountable for their outcomes can be challenging due to their complexity and opacity. However, as algorithms increasingly influence critical decisions in areas like lending, hiring, and healthcare, it becomes essential to ensure transparency and fairness. Algorithmic accountability entails understanding the impact of algorithms and establishing mechanisms to address biases and discriminatory practices.

In 2018, Amazon abandoned its AI-based hiring tool due to gender bias. The system, trained on historical resumes, penalized female candidates, reflecting the biases present in the training data. This incident highlights the importance of algorithmic accountability and the need to actively address biases.

Algorithms have a significant social impact across various domains. In healthcare, algorithms assist in diagnosis and treatment decisions, raising concerns about patient privacy and data security. In the criminal justice system, algorithms are used to assess the likelihood of reoffending, potentially perpetuating racial and socioeconomic biases.

Employment algorithms can perpetuate gender and racial biases in hiring decisions.

The Facebook-Cambridge Analytica scandal revealed how algorithms can be misused to manipulate public opinion and undermine democratic processes. It brought to light the importance of ethical considerations in algorithmic systems that handle personal data and influence political outcomes.

By understanding the ethical implications of algorithms, we can critically evaluate their impact on society. Recognizing the potential biases, we can strive to design algorithms that promote fairness, transparency, and accountability. The next section will delve into strategies to mitigate algorithmic bias and promote ethical algorithmic practices.

Mitigating Algorithmic Bias and Promoting Fairness

As algorithms play an increasingly prominent role in decision-making processes, it becomes crucial to address algorithmic bias and promote fairness. In this section, we will explore strategies and approaches to mitigate algorithmic bias and ensure that algorithms are designed and used ethically.

1. Data Collection and Preprocessing: Algorithmic bias often stems from biased or incomplete training data. It is essential to critically examine the data used to train algorithms and identify potential sources of bias. Data preprocessing techniques can help mitigate bias by removing sensitive attributes, balancing the representation of different groups, or using techniques such as oversampling and undersampling.

Pseudo Code Example:

```
// Data Preprocessing
preprocessData(data):
    // Remove sensitive attributes
    data.removeColumn("race")

    // Balance the representation of different groups
    data.oversampleMinorityGroup("gender")

    // Normalize the data
    data.normalize("age")
```

Regular Evaluation and Auditing

Regular evaluation and auditing of algorithms can help identify and rectify bias. It involves monitoring the performance of algorithms over time, measuring their impact on different groups, and assessing whether they align with ethical and legal standards. Auditing should be an ongoing process to ensure that algorithms continue to function fairly and without discrimination.

The city of Los Angeles conducted an audit of its predictive policing algorithm to assess its impact on communities. The audit revealed that the algorithm disproportionately targeted minority neighborhoods, prompting the city to reevaluate and modify its policing strategies.

Ethical Design and Development

Ethical considerations should be an integral part of algorithm design and development. It involves actively identifying potential biases, understanding the context in which algorithms will be deployed, and involving diverse perspectives in the design process. Ethical guidelines and frameworks, such as the ACM Code of Ethics or the Fairness, Accountability, and Transparency in Machine Learning (FAT/ML) principles, can provide valuable guidance.

Google's AI Principles provide a framework for responsible AI development, emphasizing the importance of avoiding bias, ensuring transparency, and promoting user benefit.

These principles guide Google's approach to AI applications across various domains.

User Empowerment and Transparency

Users should have the ability to understand and control the algorithms that impact their lives. Providing transparency about how algorithms work, the data they use, and the decision-making processes they employ can empower users to make informed choices. User feedback and recourse mechanisms should also be in place to address concerns and rectify potential biases.

The European Union's General Data Protection Regulation (GDPR) grants individuals the right to know and contest decisions made by automated systems. This regulatory framework promotes transparency and user empowerment in the context of algorithmic decision-making.

By implementing these strategies, we can mitigate algorithmic bias and promote fairness in algorithmic decision-making. It is crucial to continually assess and improve algorithms to ensure that they align with ethical standards and serve the best interests of individuals and society as a whole.

11

Real-World Applications

In this chapter, we will delve into various real-world applications of algorithmic thinking across different domains. We will explore how algorithmic principles and techniques are applied in fields such as data science, artificial intelligence, and cryptography. Through these examples, we will gain a deeper understanding of how algorithms power innovations and drive technological advancements.

Data Science

Data science is a rapidly growing field that relies heavily on algorithmic thinking to extract insights and knowledge from vast amounts of data. In this section, we will explore the application of algorithms in various data science tasks and examine real-life examples that demonstrate their impact.

1. Data Preprocessing:
Data preprocessing is a crucial step in data science that involves cleaning, transforming, and integrating raw data to ensure its quality and suitability for analysis. Algorithms are used to handle missing values, outliers, and noise in the data. Techniques like data imputation, outlier detection, and feature scaling are employed to prepare the data for further analysis. For instance, in a study conducted by a team of researchers at Stanford University, they used sophisticated algorithms to clean and preprocess a large dataset of medical records, enabling them to extract valuable insights for disease prediction and treatment planning.

2. Feature Selection:
Feature selection is the process of identifying the most relevant and informative features from a dataset. Algorithms are employed to evaluate the importance of features and select the subset that contributes the most to the predictive power of a model. This helps in reducing dimensionality and improving the model's performance. A notable real-life application is in the field of image

recognition, where algorithms are used to automatically select the most discriminative features from images, enabling accurate and efficient object recognition.

3. Predictive Modeling:
Predictive modeling involves building models that can make predictions or classifications based on historical data. Algorithms such as decision trees, random forests, and support vector machines are commonly used for this task. For example, Netflix utilizes predictive modeling algorithms to recommend personalized movie and TV show recommendations to its users based on their viewing history and preferences. By analyzing patterns in user behavior, the algorithms can accurately predict and suggest content that aligns with individual tastes.

4. Clustering:
Clustering is a technique used to group similar data points together based on their characteristics or patterns. Algorithms like k-means clustering, hierarchical clustering, and DBSCAN are employed for this purpose. Clustering algorithms find applications in various domains, such as customer segmentation, image segmentation, and anomaly detection. One remarkable application is in social network analysis, where clustering algorithms can identify communities or groups of individuals with similar interests or behaviors, facilitating targeted marketing campaigns and social network analysis.

These are just a few examples of how algorithms are used

in data science. The field is vast and ever-expanding, with new algorithms and techniques constantly being developed to tackle complex data problems. By harnessing the power of algorithms, data scientists are able to extract valuable insights, make accurate predictions, and drive data-driven decision-making across industries.

Artificial Intelligence

Artificial Intelligence (AI) is a fascinating field that relies heavily on algorithms to mimic human intelligence and perform tasks such as natural language processing, computer vision, and decision-making. In this section, we will explore real-world applications of AI and how algorithms play a crucial role in powering these advancements.

Natural Language Processing (NLP)

NLP is a branch of AI that focuses on enabling computers to understand and process human language. Algorithms such as recurrent neural networks (RNNs) and transformer models like BERT have revolutionized NLP applications. One notable example is virtual assistants like Siri, Alexa, and Google Assistant, which use sophisticated NLP algorithms to understand spoken commands, answer questions, and perform tasks like setting reminders or playing music. These algorithms employ techniques such as named entity recognition, sentiment analysis, and machine translation to process and interpret human language.

Computer Vision

Computer vision involves algorithms that enable machines to understand and interpret visual information from images and videos. Deep learning techniques, such as convolutional neural networks (CNNs), have significantly advanced computer vision applications. One remarkable real-life application is autonomous vehicles. Algorithms process real-time video feeds from cameras and use object detection, image segmentation, and tracking algorithms to identify pedestrians, vehicles, and road signs, enabling safe navigation and autonomous driving. This technology has the potential to revolutionize transportation and improve road safety.

Recommendation Systems

Recommendation systems are widely used in e-commerce, streaming platforms, and social media to personalize content recommendations to users. Collaborative filtering algorithms, content-based filtering, and hybrid approaches are employed to analyze user preferences, historical data, and item characteristics to make accurate recommendations. For example, Amazon uses recommendation algorithms to suggest products based on users' browsing and purchasing history, improving user experience and boosting sales.

Fraud Detection

Fraud detection algorithms leverage machine learning techniques to identify patterns and anomalies in data that may indicate fraudulent activity. These algorithms analyze large datasets of transactional data and detect abnormal behaviors, suspicious transactions, and potential fraud patterns. Financial institutions, such as banks and credit card companies, employ these algorithms to detect and prevent fraudulent transactions, protecting customers' financial assets and ensuring secure transactions.

These examples demonstrate how algorithms power real-world applications of artificial intelligence. As AI continues to evolve, algorithms will play a pivotal role in improving efficiency, accuracy, and decision-making across various domains.

Cryptography

Cryptography is the science of secure communication and plays a critical role in protecting sensitive information in various digital systems. In this section, we will explore real-world applications of cryptography and the algorithms that underpin secure communication.

Encryption and Decryption

Encryption algorithms are used to convert plaintext into ciphertext, ensuring that the information remains secure during transmission or storage. Decryption algorithms, on the other hand, transform the ciphertext back into its original plaintext form. One of the most widely used encryption algorithms is the Advanced Encryption Standard (AES). AES has been adopted by governments, organizations, and individuals worldwide for secure

Cryptography is the science of secure communication and plays a critical role in protecting sensitive information in various digital systems. In this section, we will explore real-world applications of cryptography and the algorithms that underpin secure communication.

Encryption and Decryption
Encryption algorithms are used to convert plaintext into ciphertext, ensuring that the information remains secure during transmission or storage. Decryption algorithms, on the other hand, transform the ciphertext back into its original plaintext form. One of the most widely used encryption algorithms is the Advanced Encryption Standard (AES). AES has been adopted by governments, organizations, and individuals worldwide for secure communication, file encryption, and data protection. Pseudo code example of AES encryption and decryption:

```
# AES encryption
key = generate_random_key()
ciphertext = aes_encrypt(plaintext, key)

# AES decryption
plaintext = aes_decrypt(ciphertext, key)
```

Digital Signatures

Digital signatures provide a means of ensuring the authenticity and integrity of digital documents or messages. These signatures are generated using asymmetric encryption algorithms such as RSA (Rivest-Shamir-Adleman). The private key is used to sign the document, while the corresponding public key is used to verify the signature. Digital signatures are extensively used in areas such as electronic transactions, secure email communication, and software distribution to ensure that the information has not been tampered with and originates from a trusted source.

Secure Hash Functions

Secure hash functions generate fixed-length hash values from input data of arbitrary size. These hash functions are designed to be computationally difficult to reverse or find collisions, making them ideal for verifying the integrity of data. The SHA-2 family of hash functions, including SHA-256, is widely used for data integrity checks, password storage, and digital certificates. Pseudo code example of SHA-256 hash function:

```
# SHA-256 hash function
hash_value = sha256(input_data)
```

Secure Communication Protocols

Cryptographic algorithms are the backbone of secure communication protocols such as Transport Layer Security (TLS). TLS is widely used to secure web communication, ensuring that data exchanged between clients and servers remains confidential and tamper-proof. TLS employs symmetric encryption algorithms for data encryption, asymmetric encryption algorithms for key exchange, and digital certificates for server authentication [4].

Real-life stories highlight the importance of cryptography in safeguarding sensitive information. One notable example is the case of Edward Snowden, a former NSA contractor who leaked classified documents revealing mass surveillance programs. The use of encryption algorithms, such as AES and RSA, would have made it significantly more difficult for unauthorized individuals to access and decrypt the leaked information.

Cryptography continues to play a vital role in protecting digital privacy, securing financial transactions, and ensuring the integrity of communication systems. The advancement of cryptography algorithms and protocols is crucial to staying ahead of evolving threats and maintaining secure digital environments.

Optimization Problems

Optimization problems are pervasive in various domains, ranging from engineering and logistics to finance and resource allocation. These problems involve finding the best solution from a set of possible solutions, considering certain constraints and objectives. In this section, we will explore real-life applications of optimization problems and how algorithms can help find optimal solutions.

Traveling Salesman Problem

The Traveling Salesman Problem (TSP) is a classic optimization problem that seeks to find the shortest possible route for a salesman who must visit a set of cities and return to the starting city, while visiting each city exactly once. Despite its simple formulation, the TSP is known to be an NP-hard problem, meaning that finding the exact optimal solution for large instances becomes computationally infeasible.

The TSP finds applications in various industries, such as transportation and logistics. For example, delivery companies often face the challenge of finding the most efficient route to deliver packages to multiple destinations. By applying TSP algorithms, they can optimize their delivery routes, reducing travel time and fuel costs.

Pseudo code example for solving the TSP using a brute-force approach:

```
function tsp(cities):
    shortest_route = None
    shortest_distance = infinity

    for each permutation in all_permutations(cities):
        distance = calculate_total_distance(permutation)
        if distance < shortest_distance:
            shortest_distance = distance
            shortest_route = permutation

    return shortest_route, shortest_distance
```

Resource Allocation

Optimization problems also arise in resource allocation scenarios where limited resources must be allocated to various tasks or individuals in an optimal manner. For example, in project management, assigning tasks to team members while considering their skills, availability, and workload can be formulated as a resource allocation problem.

Optimization algorithms, such as linear programming or integer programming, can be used to solve resource allocation problems. These algorithms find the best assignment of resources to maximize efficiency and minimize costs. In real-life situations, this can lead to improved resource utilization and better overall project performance.

Portfolio Optimization
In the field of finance, portfolio optimization aims to find the best allocation of investments to maximize returns while considering risk. Investors face the challenge of allocating their capital across various assets, such as stocks, bonds, and commodities, to achieve their desired financial goals.

Optimization techniques, such as mean-variance optimization or modern portfolio theory, can assist investors in constructing optimal investment portfolios. These algorithms analyze historical data, return rates, and correlations between assets to identify the optimal asset allocation that balances risk and return.

UPS and the "Right Turn" Strategy
United Parcel Service (UPS), one of the largest package delivery companies, optimized its delivery routes using algorithms to minimize left turns. By designing routes that mainly involve right turns, UPS was able to save millions of gallons of fuel, reduce emissions, and improve overall operational efficiency. This real-life example demonstrates the practical impact of optimization techniques in large-scale logistics operations.

Google's PageRank Algorithm
Google's PageRank algorithm is an example of using optimization to improve search engine results. The algorithm assigns a numerical score to web pages based on their importance and relevance. By optimizing the

ranking of search results, Google provides users with more accurate and useful information. The PageRank algorithm revolutionized web search and propelled Google to become the dominant search engine.

Computational Biology

Computational biology is an interdisciplinary field that combines biology, computer science, mathematics, and statistics to solve complex biological problems. It involves the development and application of algorithms to analyze biological data, model biological processes, and make discoveries in areas such as genomics, proteomics, and drug discovery. In this section, we will explore the real-life applications of computational biology and how algorithms play a crucial role in advancing our understanding of the biological world.

Genomic Sequencing and Assembly

Genomic sequencing is the process of determining the complete DNA sequence of an organism's genome. It has revolutionized biological research and medical diagnostics by providing insights into genetic variations, disease mechanisms, and evolutionary relationships. However, sequencing technologies generate massive amounts of raw data that need to be processed and assembled into a coherent genome.

Bioinformatics algorithms play a crucial role in the assembly of genomic sequences from short DNA fragments. One popular algorithm for genome assembly is the de novo assembly algorithm, which reconstructs the complete genome sequence without relying on a reference genome. These algorithms employ techniques such as overlap graph construction, read alignment, and graph traversal to piece together the puzzle of the genome.

The Human Genome Project, a monumental international effort, aimed to sequence and assemble the entire human genome. Completed in 2003, it represented a significant milestone in computational biology. The project involved the development of advanced algorithms and computational methods to handle the enormous amount of sequencing data and assemble the human genome accurately. The successful completion of the Human Genome Project has opened new avenues for understanding genetic diseases, personalized medicine, and evolutionary biology.

Protein Folding and Structure Prediction

Proteins are essential molecules in living organisms, and their functions are closely related to their three-dimensional structures. Predicting the 3D structure of a protein from its amino acid sequence is a challenging problem with significant implications for understanding protein function, drug design, and disease mechanisms.

Computational algorithms, such as molecular dynamics simulations and protein structure prediction algorithms, play a crucial role in predicting protein structures. These algorithms use mathematical and physical models to simulate the folding process and predict the most stable conformation of a protein. Machine learning techniques, such as deep learning, have also been applied to improve the accuracy of protein structure prediction.

AlphaFold and Protein Folding
DeepMind's AlphaFold is a groundbreaking deep learning algorithm that excels in predicting protein structures. In 2020, AlphaFold demonstrated exceptional accuracy in the Critical Assessment of Protein Structure Prediction (CASP) competition, outperforming other methods by a significant margin. This breakthrough has the potential to revolutionize our understanding of protein structure and function, enabling advancements in drug discovery and personalized medicine.

Pseudo code example for protein structure prediction using molecular dynamics simulation:

```
function predict_protein_structure(sequence):
    initialize_protein_structure(sequence)
    initialize_simulation_parameters()

    for each time step:
        calculate_forces()
        update_atom_positions()

    return final_protein_structure
```

Drug Discovery and Design

Computational algorithms play a vital role in drug discovery and design processes. They assist in identifying potential drug targets, screening large chemical databases for potential drug candidates, and optimizing drug molecules for efficacy and safety. These algorithms employ techniques such as molecular docking, virtual screening, and quantitative structure-activity relationship (QSAR) modeling.

By leveraging computational approaches, researchers can reduce the time and cost associated with traditional trial-and-error methods in drug discovery. They can prioritize the most promising drug candidates and optimize their chemical properties for effective targeting of specific diseases.

Computer-Aided Drug Design

Computer-aided drug design has had a significant impact on the pharmaceutical industry. For example, the development of antiretroviral drugs for HIV/AIDS treatment relied heavily on computational approaches. By analyzing the structure of viral proteins and designing inhibitors using computational algorithms, researchers have been able to develop highly effective antiretroviral drugs, improving the quality of life for millions of people living with HIV/AIDS.

Pseudo code example for molecular docking:

```
function perform_molecular_docking(target_protein, candidate_drug):
  initialize_docking_parameters()

  generate_candidate_conformations(candidate_drug)

  for each conformation:
    score = calculate_docking_score(target_protein, conformation)
    if score exceeds threshold:
      return conformation

  return null
```

Financial Modeling

Financial modeling involves the application of algorithms and mathematical models to analyze and predict financial data, make investment decisions, and assess the risk and profitability of financial instruments. It plays a critical role in various areas of finance, including investment banking, portfolio management, risk management, and quantitative trading. In this section, we will explore the real-life applications of financial modeling and how algorithms are used to analyze financial data and make informed decisions.

Modern portfolio theory, developed by Harry Markowitz, provides a mathematical framework for portfolio optimization. Algorithms such as mean-variance optimization use historical data and statistical models to determine the optimal allocation of assets in a portfolio. These algorithms aim to find the balance between risk and return by considering the covariance matrix of asset returns and the investor's risk preferences.

The Capital Asset Pricing Model (CAPM) is a widely used financial model that helps investors determine the expected return of an investment based on its risk. CAPM considers the risk-free rate of return, the market risk premium, and the asset's beta, which measures its sensitivity to market movements. By applying the CAPM formula and analyzing historical data, investors can make informed decisions about the expected returns and risks associated with different investments.

Pseudo code example for mean-variance portfolio optimization:

```
function optimize_portfolio(assets, expected_returns, covariance_matrix):
    initialize_weights(assets)
    calculate_expected_portfolio_returns(assets, expected_returns, weights)
    calculate_portfolio_variance(assets, covariance_matrix, weights)

    maximize(expected_returns, portfolio_variance)

    return optimized_weights
```

Risk Management

Risk management is a crucial aspect of financial modeling, aimed at identifying, assessing, and mitigating potential risks in investment portfolios and financial transactions. Algorithms are used to quantify and manage risks, such as market risk, credit risk, and operational risk.

Value at Risk (VaR) is a commonly used risk measure that quantifies the maximum potential loss an investment portfolio or financial instrument could experience within a given confidence level. VaR algorithms employ statistical models and historical data to estimate the potential losses under different market conditions.

The collapse of Long-Term Capital Management (LTCM) in 1998 serves as a cautionary tale about the importance of risk management. LTCM, a hedge fund managed by renowned financial experts, heavily relied on complex financial models and algorithms to identify arbitrage opportunities. However, the fund underestimated the risks associated with its investments, resulting in massive losses and near-collapse. This event highlighted the importance of sound risk management practices and the limitations of relying solely on mathematical models.

Pseudo code example for Value at Risk calculation:

```
function calculate_var(portfolio_returns, confidence_level):
  sort_returns(portfolio_returns)
  percentile = calculate_percentile(confidence_level)
  var = portfolio_returns[percentile]

  return var
```

12

Cultivating an Algorithmic Mindset

Throughout your journey of developing an algorithmic mindset, you have embarked on a transformative path that has expanded your problem-solving abilities and shaped your decision-making processes. By embracing algorithmic thinking, you have gained a valuable set of skills that empower you to tackle complex challenges with efficiency and precision.

Algorithmic thinking is not limited to computer science; it is a mindset that permeates various aspects of life. It involves breaking down problems into smaller, more manageable tasks, analyzing patterns and structures, and designing effective solutions. This systematic approach allows you to approach problems with clarity and develop logical strategies to overcome obstacles.

Reflecting on your journey, you may recall instances where algorithmic thinking has brought significant breakthroughs. Consider a real-life story of Jane, a high school teacher, who struggled with managing her classroom. Overwhelmed by the diverse needs and behaviors of her students, Jane decided to apply algorithmic thinking to create a structured behavior management system. By breaking down the problem, identifying patterns, and implementing a step-by-step approach, she was able to establish clear expectations, reward positive behaviors, and address issues systematically. As a result, the classroom environment improved, and students' learning outcomes flourished.

Recognizing Personal Growth

As you developed your algorithmic mindset, you have experienced significant personal growth. The ability to think critically, analyze data, and make informed decisions has become second nature to you. This growth extends beyond technical skills and encompasses valuable qualities such as patience, perseverance, and adaptability.

Reflect on how algorithmic thinking has influenced your problem-solving abilities. Consider a time when you tackled a challenging programming project. Initially, you may have felt overwhelmed by the complexity of the problem. However, by breaking it down into smaller sub-problems and applying algorithmic techniques, such as dynamic programming or divide and conquer, you were able to devise an elegant solution. This experience showcases how algorithmic thinking enhances your ability to approach complex tasks with confidence and navigate through intricate problem spaces.

Learning from Mistakes

Mistakes and setbacks are an inherent part of the learning process. Throughout your journey, you may have encountered numerous challenges and faced moments of frustration. However, these experiences have shaped you into a resilient problem solver.

Realize that mistakes are not failures but opportunities for growth. Remember the time when you encountered a bug in your code that resulted in unexpected behavior. Instead of becoming disheartened, you embraced the challenge as a chance to improve your debugging skills and enhance your understanding of the programming language. By meticulously analyzing the issue, identifying the root cause, and implementing corrective measures, you eventually overcame the problem. This experience exemplifies the importance of perseverance, patience, and the ability to learn from mistakes.

Nurturing Algorithmic Thinking in Daily Life

Algorithmic thinking is not limited to the realm of computer science; it can be applied to various aspects of our daily lives. By cultivating an algorithmic mindset, you can enhance your problem-solving skills, optimize your decision-making processes, and find innovative solutions to everyday challenges.

In your personal life, algorithmic thinking can help you manage your time more efficiently. Consider the story of John, a busy professional who struggled to balance his work and personal commitments. Faced with numerous tasks and limited time, John decided to apply algorithmic thinking to prioritize his activities. He analyzed the importance and urgency of each task, identified dependencies and potential bottlenecks, and developed a systematic schedule to maximize productivity. Through this approach, John was able to optimize his time management and achieve a better work-life balance.

Algorithmic thinking can also be beneficial in financial decision-making. Let's imagine Sarah, a young professional saving for her dream vacation. Sarah employed algorithmic thinking to create a budgeting system that analyzed her income, expenses, and savings goals. By identifying spending patterns, setting financial targets, and making informed choices based on algorithms, Sarah successfully managed to save enough money for her vacation within a specific timeframe. This real-life example illustrates how algorithmic thinking can empower individuals to make sound financial decisions and achieve their goals.

Pseudo Code Example: Applying Algorithmic Thinking to Time Management

```
function optimizeTimeManagement(tasks):
    sortedTasks = sortTasksByPriority(tasks)
    schedule = []
    currentTime = 0

    for task in sortedTasks:
        if currentTime + task.duration <= MAX_TIME:
            schedule.append(task)
            currentTime += task.duration

    return schedule
```

In the above pseudo code example, we define a function `optimizeTimeManagement` that takes a list of tasks as input. The function sorts the tasks by priority, iterates over them, and adds them to the schedule as long as the allocated time (`currentTime`) does not exceed the maximum time available (`MAX_TIME`). This algorithmic approach ensures that tasks are prioritized and efficiently scheduled, allowing for optimal time management.

Conclusion

Congratulations! You have now completed the journey of exploring the algorithmic mindset. Throughout this book, we have delved into the world of algorithms, their design patterns, ethical implications, real-world applications, and strategies to cultivate algorithmic thinking in your daily life. By embracing this mindset, you have gained a powerful tool for problem-solving, decision-making, and innovation.

As we conclude this book, let's reflect on the key takeaways and the impact of algorithmic thinking:

Problem-Solving Power: Algorithmic thinking equips you with the ability to break down complex problems into smaller, more manageable tasks. By approaching problems systematically, you can develop effective algorithms to solve them efficiently.

Creative Solutions: Algorithmic thinking encourages you to think outside the box and find innovative solutions. By examining problems from different angles and applying algorithmic design patterns, you can come up with creative approaches that lead to breakthroughs.

Ethical Considerations: Algorithms have a profound impact on society, influencing various aspects of our lives. It is crucial to be aware of the ethical implications, such as algorithmic bias and privacy concerns. By understanding these issues, you can strive for fairness and responsibility in algorithmic decision-making.

Real-World Applications: Algorithms are the driving force behind technological advancements. They power fields such as data science, artificial intelligence, finance, and more. By exploring real-life examples and case studies, you have witnessed the immense potential of algorithmic thinking in these domains.

Continuous Growth: Cultivating an algorithmic mindset is an ongoing journey. It requires curiosity, practice, and an open mind. As technology evolves, new algorithmic challenges and opportunities will arise, and your mindset will continue to expand and adapt.

Remember, algorithmic thinking is not solely for computer scientists or mathematicians. It is a mindset that anyone can develop and apply in their own unique way. By incorporating algorithmic thinking into your daily life, you can become a more effective problem-solver, decision-maker, and contributor to the advancement of society.

Pseudo Code Example: Continuously Nurturing Algorithmic Thinking

```
function nurtureAlgorithmicThinking():
  while true:
    learn new algorithms and data structures
    solve algorithmic puzzles and challenges
    explore algorithmic applications in different fields
    engage in algorithmic discussions and communities
    reflect on algorithmic approaches to real-life problems
```

The above pseudo code example represents a continuous loop of nurturing algorithmic thinking. It emphasizes the importance of ongoing learning, problem-solving, exploration, and reflection. By immersing yourself in algorithmic activities and staying connected with the algorithmic community, you can foster and nourish your algorithmic mindset.

In conclusion, the journey of developing an algorithmic mindset is an exciting and empowering one. By embracing algorithmic thinking, you have gained a powerful set of tools and skills to navigate the challenges of the digital age. Remember to apply these principles ethically, consider the impact of algorithms on society, and continue to explore and expand your algorithmic horizons. May your algorithmic mindset guide you to new discoveries, innovative solutions, and a deeper understanding of the world around you.

References

- Cormen, T. H., Leiserson, C. E., Rivest, R. L., & Stein, C. (2009). Introduction to Algorithms. MIT Press.

- Grover, S., & Pea, R. (2013). Computational thinking in K-12: A review of the state of the field. Educational researcher, 42(1), 38-43.

- The Netflix Prize. (n.d.). Retrieved from https://netflixprize.com/

- Kumar, S. (2017). Algorithmic Thinking: Building Blocks for Computational Problem Solving. CRC Press.

- Cormen, T. H., Leiserson, C. E., Rivest, R. L., & Stein, C. (2009). Introduction to Algorithms. MIT Press.
- - Levitin, A. (2012). Introduction to the Design and Analysis of Algorithms. Pearson.

- Witten, I. H., Frank, E., Hall, M. A., & Pal, C. J. (2016). Data Mining: Practical Machine Learning Tools and Techniques. Morgan Kaufmann.

- Szeliski, R. (2010). Computer Vision: Algorithms and Applications. Springer.

References - 218

- O'Neil, C. (2016). Weapons of Math Destruction: How Big Data Increases Inequality and Threatens Democracy. Crown.

- Buolamwini, J., & Gebru, T. (2018). Gender Shades: Intersectional Accuracy Disparities in Commercial Gender Classification. Proceedings of the 1st Conference on Fairness, Accountability and Transparency, 77-91.

- Russell, S., & Norvig, P. (2016). Artificial Intelligence: A Modern Approach. Pearson.

- Preskill, J. (2018). Quantum Computing in the NISQ era and beyond. Quantum, 2, 79.

- Cormen, T. H., Leiserson, C. E., Rivest, R. L., & Stein, C. (2009). Introduction to Algorithms (3rd ed.). MIT Press.

- Kleinberg, J., & Tardos, E. (2005). Algorithm Design. Pearson.

- Russell, S. J., & Norvig, P. (2016). Artificial Intelligence: A Modern Approach (3rd ed.). Pearson.

- Cormen, T. H., Leiserson, C. E., Rivest, R. L., & Stein, C. (2009). Introduction to Algorithms (3rd ed.). MIT Press.

- Dasgupta, S., Papadimitriou, C. H., & Vazirani, U. V. (2006). Algorithms. McGraw-Hill.

- Skiena, S. S. (2008). The Algorithm Design Manual (2nd ed.). Springer.

- Cormen, T. H., Leiserson, C. E., Rivest, R. L., & Stein, C. (2009). Introduction to Algorithms (3rd ed.). MIT Press.

- Williamson, D. P., & Shmoys, D. B. (2011). The Design of Approximation Algorithms. Cambridge University Press

- European Commission. (n.d.). Data protection.

- Google. (n.d.). AI at Google: Our Approach.

- Levitin, A. (2012). Algorithmic Thinking: A Problem-Based Introduction. Wiley.

- Grover, S., & Pea, R. (2013). Computational Thinking in K-12: A Review of the State of the Field. Educational Researcher, 42(1), 38-43.

- - Cormen, T. H., Leiserson, C. E., Rivest, R. L., & Stein, C. (2009). Introduction to Algorithms. MIT Press.

- Wilkerson, B. L., & Shah, N. B. (2016). Computational Thinking: A Definition. In Proceedings of the 2016 ITiCSE Working Group Reports (pp. 57-74).

- Denning, P. J. (2009). Beyond Calculation: The Next Fifty Years of Computing. Communications of the ACM, 52(1), 30-32.

- Sedgewick, R., & Wayne, K. (2011). Algorithms (4th ed.). Addison-Wesley Professional.

- Lafore, R. (2002). Data Structures and Algorithms in Java (2nd ed.). Sams Publishing.

- - Sedgewick, R., & Wayne, K. (2011). Algorithms (4th ed.). Addison-Wesley Professional.

- Weiss, M. A. (2013). Data Structures and Algorithm Analysis in Java (3rd ed.). Pearson.

- Cormen, T. H., Leiserson, C. E., Rivest, R. L., & Stein, C. (2009). Introduction to Algorithms (3rd ed.). MIT Press.

- Sedgewick, R., & Wayne, K. (2011). Algorithms (4th ed.). Addison-Wesley Professional.

- Angwin, J., Larson, J., Mattu, S., & Kirchner, L. (2016). Machine Bias. ProPublica.

- Cadwalladr, C. (2018). The great British Brexit robbery: How our democracy was hijacked. The Guardian.

- Caliskan, A., Bryson, J. J., & Narayanan, A. (2017). Semantics derived automatically from language corpora contain human-like biases. Science.

For the Better.

- Antonio Scapellato -

H&N

HACKERS AND NERDS

H&N

H&N

H&N

Unleash Your Problem-Solving Potential with "Algorithmic Mindset"!

Discover the power of algorithms and cultivate an algorithmic mindset with Antonio Scapellato's captivating book. Through twelve chapters, explore the fundamentals of algorithmic thinking, problem-solving strategies, data structures, and algorithm efficiency. Delve into recursion, sorting and searching algorithms, graph theory, computational thinking, algorithm design patterns, ethical implications, real-world applications, and nurturing an algorithmic mindset. With engaging examples and practical insights, this book equips you to conquer challenges and embrace the algorithmic mindset.

—— **Antonio Scapellato**

www.ingramcontent.com/pod-product-compliance
Lightning Source LLC
LaVergne TN
LVHW051321050326
832903LV00031B/3290